CW00501532

Sacred Fife and the Forth Valley

SACRED PLACES SERIES

Sacred Fife and the Forth Valley

SCOTLAND'S CHURCHES SCHEME

SAINT ANDREW PRESS
Edinburgh

First published in 2009 by
SAINT ANDREW PRESS
121 George Street
Edinburgh
EH2 4YN

Copyright Text © Scotland's Churches Scheme, 2009
Copyright *Pilgrimage* article © Ian Bradley, 2009
Copyright *Sacred Fife and the Forth Valley* article © John Hume, 2009
Copyright maps © Jim Lewis, 2009
Colour photographs used in this book are copyright and are used with the permission
of the Royal Commission on the Ancient and Historical Monuments of Scotland;
Professor John R. Hume and Mr A. Stewart Brown.

ISBN 978 0 7152 0923 3

All rights reserved. No part of this publication may be reproduced or transmitted in
any form or by any means, electronic or mechanical, including photocopy, recording,
or information storage and retrieval system, without permission in writing from the
publisher. This book is sold subject to the condition that it shall not, by way of trade
or otherwise, be lent, resold, hired out or otherwise circulated without the publisher's
prior consent.

The right of Scotland's Churches Scheme to be identified as author of this work has
been asserted in accordance with the Copyright, Designs and Patents Act 1988.

British Library Cataloguing in Publication Data
A catalogue record for this book is available from the British Library.

It is the publisher's policy to only use papers that are natural and recyclable and that
have been manufactured from timber grown in renewable, properly managed forests.
All of the manufacturing processes of the papers are expected to conform to the
environmental regulations of the country of origin.

Typeset in Enigma by Waverley Typesetters, Fakenham
Manufactured in Great Britain by Bell & Bain Ltd, Glasgow

BUCKINGHAM PALACE

As Patron of Scotland's Churches Scheme I warmly welcome this publication, particularly during this year of *Homecoming Scotland 2009*.

The story of the heritage and culture of Scotland would be lacking significantly without a strong focus on its churches and sacred sites. I am sure that this guidebook will be a source of information and enjoyment both to the people of Scotland and to our visitors during this memorable year.

Anne

Scotland's Churches Scheme

Scotland's Churches Scheme is an ecumenical charitable trust, providing an opportunity to access the nation's living heritage of faith by assisting the 'living' churches to:

- Promote spiritual understanding by enabling the public to appreciate all buildings designed for worship and active as living churches
- Work together with others to make the Church the focus of the community
- Open their doors with a welcoming presence
- Tell the story of the building (however old or new), its purpose and heritage (artistic, architectural and historical)
- Provide information for visitors, young and old

The Scheme has grown rapidly since its inception in 1994 and there are now more than 1200 churches in membership. These churches are spread across Scotland and across the denominations.

The *Sacred Scotland* theme promoted by Scotland's Churches Scheme focuses on the wish of both visitors and local communities to be able to access our wonderful range of church buildings in a meaningful way, whether the visit be occasioned by spiritual or heritage motivation or both. The Scheme can advise and assist member churches on visitor welcome, and with its range of 'how-to' brochures, provide information on research, presentation, security and other live issues. The Scheme, with its network of local representatives, encourages the opening of doors, the care of tourists and locals alike, and offers specific services such as the provision of grants for organ playing.

Sacred Scotland (www.sacredscotland.org.uk), the web-site of Scotland's Churches Scheme, opens the door to Scotland's story by exploring living traditions of faith in city, town, village and island across the country. The site is a portal to access information on Scotland's churches of all denominations and a starting point for your special journeys.

We are delighted to be working with Saint Andrew Press in the publication of this series of regional guides to Scotland's churches. This volume, *Fife and the Forth Valley*, is one of three being published in 2009 (the others are *Edinburgh and Midlothian* and *South-West Scotland*) to be followed by a further three books in 2010 and again in 2011 when the whole country will have been covered. We are grateful to the authors of the introductory articles, Professor John Hume, one of our Trustees, and Ian Bradley for their expert contributions to our understanding of sacred places.

The growth of 'spiritual tourism' worldwide is reflected in the million-plus people who visit Scotland's religious sites annually. We hope that the information in this book will be useful in bringing alive the heritage as well as the ministry of welcome which our churches offer. In the words of our President, Lady Marion Fraser: 'we all owe a deep debt of gratitude to the many people of vision who work hard and imaginatively to create a lasting and peaceful atmosphere which you will carry away with you as a special memory when you leave'.

DR BRIAN FRASER
Director

Invitation to Pilgrimage

Fife and the Forth Valley

The area covered in this guide is rich in associations with early Scottish saints. St Serf, who according to one legend began his ministry at Culross where he fostered the infant St Kentigern, seems to have spent much of his life evangelising around the Ochil Hills, with a preaching base at Loch Airte. A well at Alva, a bridge in the Glendevon Valley and an island in Loch Leven are all dedicated to this shadowy but significant foundational figure in the history of Christianity in Scotland. St Ninian is said in some accounts to have got as far east as Stirling in his missionary journeys from his base at Whithorn. Dedications to St Fillan at Aberdour and Pittenweem suggest that this eighth-century Irish saint may possibly have visited and evangelised the Fife coast from his base around Loch Earn.

The saint who dominates the ecclesiastical history of this area, however, is one who never set foot in Scotland but who was taken up in the Middle Ages as the nation's patron and protector. According to a legend which surfaced in the late eighth or early ninth century, the relics of the apostle Andrew were brought to the east coast of Scotland by a monk named Regulus or Rule in the fourth century. They were installed first in St Rule's church, the tower of which remains a prominent landmark for sailors and fishermen, and later in the magnificent cathedral built between 1160 and 1318. The supposed relics of the apostle attracted pilgrims from across Europe who flocked to the small and remote town on the East Neuk of Fife which took the apostle's name. Although it never achieved the popularity of Rome or Santiago di Compostella, St Andrews became one of the leading pilgrimage destinations in medieval Europe and as a result gained supremacy in the Scottish church and acquired its University, the third oldest in Britain after Oxford and Cambridge.

The heyday of pilgrimage to St Andrews was from the mid twelfth to the early sixteenth centuries. The whole town was laid out to facilitate pilgrim processions with the two major streets, North Street and South Street, made deliberately wide and designed to provide a circular one-way system to ease the flow of pilgrims to and from the Cathedral. Between them ran Market Street where the numerous merchants catering for the pilgrims' physical needs were based. Their spiritual needs were met by the major religious orders who provided guest houses and hospices. The largest, dedicated to St Leonard and with special provision for lepers, was built very close to the Cathedral. The Chapel associated with this hospice, substantially restored in 1904 after centuries lying derelict, is now used by the University and is the setting for a candlelit service of Compline at 10pm every Thursday evening in term-time. Nearby are the impressive remains of the medieval gates into the Cathedral precincts at the Pends, through which pilgrims would process on their way up from the harbour. A good number of pilgrims seem to have travelled by sea. In 1333 a priest from Dunkirk, found guilty of manslaughter, was sentenced by a French ecclesiastical court to make a penitential pilgrimage to St Andrews. He was ordered to travel alone, reflect daily on his crime, and on his arrival arrange and pay for thirteen requiem masses for the repose of the soul of the man he had killed.

For those coming to St Andrews by land from other parts of the British Isles, a network of pilgrim routes was developed across Fife. To help those coming from England and southern Scotland, Queen Margaret of Scotland established the ferry route across the River Forth between the present rail and road bridges, giving her name to the settlements at either side of the crossing, South and North Queensferry where she built pilgrim hospices. From North Queensferry, pilgrims walked to St Andrews via Inverkeithing, Loch Leven, Scotlandwell, where a major hospice was built, Markinch, Kennoway and Ceres. Another much longer ferry passage across the Forth estuary was established by the Earl of Dunbar between North Berwick and Earlsferry, near Elie, a distance of over 32km (20 miles). Cistercian nuns set up hospices at either end of this crossing from where they supervised the manufacture and sale of pilgrim badges.

Pilgrims coming from west and central Scotland travelled via Perth and took a ferry across the River Tay where it is joined by the Earn, while those coming from the north and east crossed the Tay estuary via Dundee and Tayport. These two routes converged to cross the River Eden by ford or ferry at the site of the modern village of Guardbridge just five miles north of St Andrews. This was often a hazardous crossing – on one occasion in the late fourteenth century twenty monks were drowned while attempting it – and in 1419 Henry Wardlaw, the Bishop of St Andrews credited with founding the University, built a stone bridge which still survives today next to the modern bridge which carries the A91 trunk road. A large hospice was set up at Guardbridge which functioned as an assembly station where pilgrims, many of whom had travelled alone or in small groups, would gather and spend their last night before walking together in procession to the apostle's shrine.

It was as a result of these and other developments that Fife became Scotland's pilgrim kingdom. So in a sense it has remained, although nowadays most of those making their way by rail or road to St Andrews are paying homage to the home of golf rather than to the apostle's relics. An enterprising ecumenical project is currently underway to revive St Andrews as a place of religious pilgrimage and interfaith understanding. Visitors to the fine Norman church of St Athernase in Leuchars will find interpretative panels about Fife's pilgrim history. In St Andrews, the Cathedral ruins are increasingly being used for religious services again and the development of a major festival around St Andrew's Day on 30 November is giving more prominence to the spiritual significance of this part of Scotland.

Although St Andrews was for centuries the most important religious centre in the area, there are other places with notable connections with the development of Christianity in Scotland. St Blane and St Serf were sixth-century Celtic missionaries who founded monasteries at Dunblane and Culross respectively, and the later St Fillan is remembered in Strathfillan and St Fillans. They are shadowy figures, unlike Queen Margaret of Scotland who founded the monastery at Dunfermline, where she was initially buried and which became a place of pilgrimage. Several key figures in post-Reformation church history also hail from Fife and the Forth Valley. Richard Cameron, Covenanting leader and martyr, was born in Falkland. His followers – the Cameronians – kept his memory alive, and their successors eventually became the Reformed Presbyterian Church. Ralph and Ebenezer Erskine, ministers in Dunfermline and Stirling, were leaders in the first Secession from the Church of Scotland in 1733. Thomas Gillespie, also a minister in Dunfermline, was one of the founders of the Relief Church, the second great eighteenth-century Secession. Thomas Chalmers, born in Anstruther, and with his first charge at Kilmany, is remembered as one of the architects of the Disruption in the Church of Scotland in 1843, which resulted in the formation of the Free Church.

It would probably be fair to say that no other part of Scotland has played such a significant role in the post-Reformation evolution of the Church in Scotland.

IAN BRADLEY
Reader in Practical Theology and Church History,
School of Divinity, University of St Andrews

Introduction

Fife and the Forth Valley

The River Forth and its Firth form a body of water which has since prehistoric times shaped settlement in south-east and central Scotland. The river and its tributaries rise in Highland Scotland, and traverse what were large areas of bog until Stirling is reached. This town is where a natural north–south route crosses the river, and also the point where the river becomes navigable. The natural rocky outcrop dominating the town was a natural site for a settlement, and in due course for a fortress. East of Stirling the river flows in a series of loops to Kincardine, where it opens out into the Firth of Forth, a vast expanse of water round which many towns formed, relying on foreign and coastal trade and on the catching of fish. The dominant place on the Firth is Edinburgh, with its castle rock similar in character and importance to that of Stirling. The land which borders the river and firth was the heart of the Kingdom of Scotland from the time of its formation in the eleventh century, and was thus the scene of many of the most significant historical events in Scottish history.

Until the coming of the railway, the water unified rather than divided the area, giving much of it a coherent character. For the most part, it is sheltered from the prevailing rain-laden westerly winds by ranges of hills, which give its eastern parts a relatively

Fig. 1. The body of St Rule's Church, St Andrews, Fife

Fig. 2. A spirelet at St Andrews Cathedral, Fife

dry climate. Most of it lies between the two boundary faults which define the Scottish Lowlands, and it has had extensive deposits of economic minerals – coal, ironstone, limestone, fireclay and oil shale. The exploitation of these has superimposed a pattern of settlement on earlier patterns, and though mineral extraction has all but ended the relic towns and villages usually survive. There was never the dense industrialisation here characteristic of west central Scotland, but there were important centres of linen manufacture in Fife, of brewing and distilling in Alloa, of iron smelting and ironfounding in the Falkirk area, and the still dominant oil-refining and petrochemicals industry of Grangemouth. All of these factors have influenced church building in the area, and the superimposition of successive layers of economically driven settlement and land use on a relatively restricted area has destroyed or obscured much of the evidence of the prehistoric and early historic use of the area, including, presumably, earlier sacred sites.

For the purpose of this volume, Edinburgh and East Lothian have been excluded from the definition 'Forth Valley', so that the local authority areas covered are, from west to east, Stirling, Clackmannanshire, Falkirk, Fife and West Lothian. The inclusion of Fife as a whole takes in North Fife, which borders the Tay and its Firth, but as Fife has been a distinct entity for centuries this seems reasonable.

The remains of prehistoric religious or ceremonial sites are not as numerous in the Forth Valley as in some other parts of Scotland, probably

Fig. 3. The tower of Cambuskenneth Abbey, Stirling

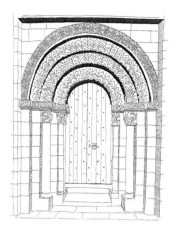

Fig. 4. The West Door, Dunfermline Abbey, Fife

because of the intensive settlement of the area since prehistoric times. Notable places which seem to have had important meanings to prehistoric settlers include the summit of Cairnpapple Hill, used for burials and other ceremonies for over a thousand years from about 2000 BC. Another very different complex, at Balfarg and Balbirnie in Fife, consisted of a stone circle and a circular platform surrounded by a ditch, with timber ritual enclosures. The meaning of these structures is obscure, as is that of the standing stones of the area. From the early historic period there are remains of Roman occupation, during which worship of the Roman pantheon would have been practised.

Much of the early Christian heritage of the area is still obscure, but there are some Pictish stones in Fife, and the remains of two Northumbrian eighth-century crosses at Abercorn, where there was a monastery from about AD 685. Further west there is place-name evidence for the activities of Irish missionaries, including dedications to St Columba, St Blane and most notably St Fillan, whose bell and crozier head are in the National Museum of Scotland in Edinburgh. There are also some simple crosses in Strathfillan, notably at Balquhidder. There is an apparently abrupt change in the eleventh century, when the area's first substantial surviving church was built: St Rule's in St Andrews (Fig. 1), apparently constructed by Culdees,

Fig. 5. Torphichen Preceptory, West Lothian

Fig. 6. St Magridin's Church, Abdie, Fife

clergy of the Celtic church, to house relics of St Andrew, probably brought here in the eighth century.

Within a century or so, however, Scotland's religious landscape had been revolutionised, largely by David I, who created a recognisably modern institutional Church, with dioceses, parishes and abbeys. The effect of this revolution can be seen very clearly in the Forth Valley, which contains some of the finest church and other religious buildings created by that institutional Church. Some of these survive as ruins, but a surprising number are still in use for worship, though most of these have been altered to some degree. In the pre-Reformation period there were two cathedrals, St Andrews (1160 on, Fig. 2) and Dunblane (**76**, thirteenth century as cathedral), and six abbeys: Balmerino (1226), Cambuskenneth (c.1140, Fig. 3), Culross (**48**, 1217), Dunfermline (c.1130, Fig. 4), Inchcolm (1235 as abbey), and Lindores (c.1191). There were also a number of lesser monastic houses, including priories at Inchmahome (c.1240) and Pittenweem (fourteenth century), and on the Isle of May (c.1145). There was a friary at Inverkeithing (fourteenth century), part of which survives. A unique building is Torphichen Preceptory (next to **119**, twelfth century and later, Fig. 5), headquarters in central Scotland of the Knights Hospitallers of the Order of St John.

In addition, this area boasts two of the greatest Scottish medieval burgh churches, the Holy Rude, Stirling (**86**, 1456 on), and St Michael's, Linlithgow (**114**, fifteenth century), and royal chapels in Linlithgow Palace (probably early 1490s), Falkland Palace (c.1540 and later) and Stirling Castle (**87**, early post-

Fig. 7. The Dunfermline Aisle, St Bridget's Church, Dalgety, Fife

Fig. 8. Kilrenny Parish Church, Fife

Reformation). Of the lesser medieval parish churches, the most distinguished are St Monan's (**26**, 1370), St Fillan's, Aberdour (**47**, early twelfth century on, restored 1925), and St Athernase, Leuchars (**16**). The latter has a twelfth-century choir and apse, which are, with the contemporary Dalmeny (see Edinburgh and Midlothian volume) and the surviving nave of Dunfermline Abbey, the finest surviving early Romanesque church buildings in Scotland. The tower of Markinch (**43**, 1150) and the tower and roofless church of St Rule, St Andrews (eleventh century), are also of this period or slightly earlier. There are other pre-Reformation towers at Inverkeithing (**55**, fourteenth century), and at Dysart St Serf's, and Kirkcaldy Old (**38**), both c.1500. Other parish churches incorporating medieval fabric include Crail (**4**, twelfth century on); Cupar Old and St Michael of Tarvit (**6**, 1415 on); Holy Trinity (**20**, 1412, restored 1909) and St Salvator's Chapel (**25**, 1460), St Andrews; St Nicholas Uphall (**120**, twelfth century on), Kirk of Calder (**117**, sixteenth century on), and Ecclesmachan, West Lothian, which has twelfth-century doorways.

After the Reformation in 1560, the abbeys and priories were disbanded, and many of the church buildings were adapted for Reformed worship, usually on a reduced scale, as elsewhere in Scotland. Of the great churches, only St Andrews Cathedral was abandoned completely, but at Dunfermline Abbey, Dunblane Cathedral and Culross Abbey only parts were retained, while the

Fig. 9. Largo and Newburn Parish Church, Fife

Fig. 10. Tulliallan Old Parish Church, Fife

Holy Rude, Stirling was split in two. Remarkably, Dunblane retains several sets of pre-Reformation stalls. The construction of new parish churches began soon after the Reformation. Early examples include Abercorn (**111**, reconstructed in 1579, and subsequently extended, and the roofless old church at Kemback (1582). The outstanding early post-Reformation church, however, is Burntisland, a burgh church on a square plan (**31**, 1592 on). There are roofless remains of a number of churches built or rebuilt in the seventeenth century such as St Magridin's, Abdie (Fig. 6), Balquhidder (1631) and Logie (1684). Most of these are probably reconstructions of pre-Reformation buildings. At St Bridget's, Dalgety (Fig. 7) the substantial Dunfermline Aisle was added in c.1610 to the twelfth-/thirteenth-century church. A phenomenon unique to Fife in the early post-Reformation period was the building or enlargement of church towers, often with short stone spires. The area's grandest seventeenth-century church is that of Anstruther Easter (**1**, 1634–44), which has such a tower, and there are others at Pittenweem (**18**, 1588, c1630), Kilrenny (fifteenth century, upper part sixteenth century, Fig. 8), Cupar Old and St Michael of Tarvit (**6**, upper part of tower 1620), and Largo and Newburn (steeple 1628, Fig. 9), all churches still in use. Similar spired towers are also to be found in a number of the tolbooths in the area. The extent of such building in stone testifies to the prosperity of the county of Fife's trading burghs in the seventeenth century. Later examples of towers are to be found at Tulliallan (1675, Fig. 10), Alloa, Clackmannanshire (1680), and most spectacularly at

Fig. 11. The former Moonzie Parish Church, Fife

Fig. 12. Kilmany Parish Church, Fife

St Ninian's Old Parish Church, Stirling (**93**, 1734).

The eighteenth century saw, throughout the area, two powerful influences on church building, agricultural improvement and the beginnings of industrialisation. The former resulted in increased prosperity in rural parishes, and the expansion of villages, and the latter was responsible for the development of towns, and the founding of new communities. With church building for the established Church of Scotland the responsibility of the landowners and burgh councils, increased population and increased prosperity led to the building of larger churches, and more elaborate ones. Some of these were centrally placed to serve a scattered farming population, others were constructed in settlements. Good examples of rural churches of the eighteenth century include Moonzie (c.1700, Fig. 11), Kilmany (1786, Fig. 12) and Cults (**5**, 1793), and of settlement churches Whitburn South (**121**, 1729–30), Falkirk Old and St Modan's (**100**, 1734), Torphichen (**119**, 1756) and Gargunnock (**82**, 1774). Some of the new eighteenth-century buildings had relatively short lives, being replaced in the nineteenth century by larger and usually more elaborate structures. Examples of this phenomenon include Killearn, Dollar and Polmont. At all of these places the roofless older church survives (1734, Fig. 13, 1774 and 1731–2 respectively). Other eighteenth-century churches have been significantly altered.

Another aspect of the Church in the eighteenth century was the splits which occurred in the established Church. The first of these was in 1733, the Original Secession, and occurred in this area. Subsequently this body split, and split again, though most of the congregations concerned came together in 1820. The second was in the

Fig. 13. Killearn Old Parish Church, Stirling

Fig. 14. Cairneyhill Church, Fife (ex Secession)

1760s, to form the Relief Church. Both of these major secessions were fundamentally about objections to the right of the 'heritors' – landowners and town councils – to appoint ministers to parish churches (patronage). The various secessions were powerful in the Forth Valley, and several of their buildings survive. The oldest is probably Edinbellie (1742), now part of a farm steading near Balfron. Cairneyhill (1752 on, Fig. 14), near Dunfermline, is still in use. Most of the others have found other uses. The end of proscription of the Scottish Episcopal Church in the later eighteenth century appears to have had little effect on the Forth Valley, as there appear to have been few families which held to the 'old religion'. The same is true of Roman Catholicism.

As a result of agricultural improvement, and of the relatively dry climate of eastern central Scotland, the Forth Valley was well-placed to take advantage of the high grain prices that resulted from the long French wars of the late eighteenth and early nineteenth centuries. The local textile industries also benefited from the blockade of the Continent for much of that period. Improvement of roads, and the construction of early railways, also favoured the accumulation of wealth. The outcome for church building was the construction of larger and more elaborate churches. Rural examples from the early nineteenth century include Ceres (**3**, 1806, spire 1852), Muiravonside (1806), Saline (**59**, 1810) and Balmerino (1811). A further impetus to church construction came with the return of servicemen from the wars. Characteristic of Scottish church architecture of the 1810s, 1820s and 1830s was what has been termed 'Heritors' Gothic' – simple early Gothic Revival buildings with bell-towers. There are good examples at Clackmannan (**62**, 1815), Kincardine in Menteith

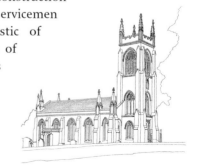

Fig. 15. Lecropt Parish Church, Stirling

Fig. 16. Limekilns Parish Church, Fife (ex United Secession)

(1816), Airth (1820), Larbert Old (**108**, 1820), Fintry (**81**, 1823) and Lecropt (1826, Fig. 15). More elaborate early Gothic Revival churches were also built during this period, as at Alloa St Mungo's (**60**, 1816–19), Dunfermline Abbey (**50**, 1821) and Kilconquhar (**15**, 1821). From the 1840s, railway building encouraged trade and industry, and the growth of towns, which became the focal points for church building. Migration of Irish Roman Catholics resulted in a demand for churches, and there was also a revival of Episcopalianism. The earliest Episcopal church in the area is probably St Columba's, Aberdour (**46**, 1843) originally a private chapel.

More important in quantitative terms were three significant changes in the organisation of the Presbyterian churches. Most of the congregations descended from the original Secession came together in 1820 as the United Secession Church, and it in turn amalgamated with the Relief Church in 1847 to form the United Presbyterian Church. This became a powerful denomination in the second half of the nineteenth century, especially in the towns. There are good examples of United Secession churches at Limekilns (1825, Fig. 16), and Kirkcaldy Linktown (**40**, 1831). The church in Colinsburgh (1843-4, Fig. 17) was built for the Relief Church, and there is a former Relief church in Cupar (1840). Even more significant than these moves was the Disruption in the Church of Scotland in 1843, when about a third of the ministers of that church walked out of the General Assembly and formed a new body, the Free Church of Scotland. The reasons for this split were complex but, as in the secessions of the eighteenth century, an important consideration was the right of the heritors to

Fig. 17. Colinsburgh Parish Church, Fife (ex Relief)

Fig. 18. Erskine United Free Church, Burntisland, Fife

appoint ministers regardless of the wishes of congregations (patronage). The new church had quickly to find resources to build new churches, manses and schools, and to pay the stipends (salaries) of ministers and schoolmasters. The first of the new churches were simple, basic structures, but as the century wore on the Free, United Presbyterian, Roman Catholic, and Scottish Episcopal churches all built churches in most towns and many villages. Most of the first generation of Free churches in the area have been demolished or converted to other uses. Good examples of conversions can be found in Saline (1844) and Clackmannan (1845). The early Free churches in Brightons (**99**, 1846–7) and Kennoway (1848) are still in use for worship. Early examples of larger Free churches include Murrayfield United Free Church, Bannockburn (1849–50) and what is now Stirling Baptist Church (1851–3).

The Church of Scotland continued to grow, but for the most part made do with its pre-Disruption buildings. A significant new building was Falkland (**12**, 1849–50). Other important Church of Scotland churches of the second half of the nineteenth century include Port of Menteith (**85**, 1876–8), Killearn (1880–2), Callander St Kessog's (1883, no longer a church), and Bo'ness Old (1885–8). In the late nineteenth century, the Church of Scotland experienced a revival based largely on the reintroduction of worship rooted in pre-Reformation patterns. New churches were built, and others altered to suit this movement, sometimes known as the Scoto-Catholic movement, which had links with the Oxford Movement in the Church of England. That movement also affected worship, and hence church design, in the Scottish Episcopal Church. Interest in the pre-Reformation Scottish Church also led to the restoration of some of the surviving medieval buildings, notably

Fig. 19. St Leonard's Parish Church, St Andrews, Fife

Dunblane Cathedral (**76**, 1889–93), St Michael's, Linlithgow (**114**, 1894–6), and Leuchars Parish Church (**16**, 1914). Scholarly study of Scots Gothic and Romanesque architecture also influenced the design of a number of late nineteenth- and early twentieth-century church buildings, including St Columba's, Stirling (1899–1902), St Leonard's, Dunfermline (**51**, 1903–4), St David's, Bathgate (1904) and Carriden (**97**, 1907–9), as well as the reconstruction of Holy Trinity, St Andrews (**20**).

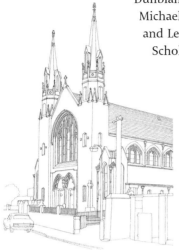

Fig. 20. St Mary's Roman Catholic Church, Bathgate, West Lothian

In the later nineteenth century, coal mining in the central Forth valley prospered, especially in west Fife. The ports of Grangemouth, Bo'ness, Burntisland and Methil were developed for the export of coal on a large scale. Manufacturing industry also boomed. The Clackmannanshire towns of Alloa, Alva and Tillicoultry, and Stirling became important centres of woollen manufacture, Alloa became a major brewing and distilling centre, and Kirkcaldy and Dunfermline prospered as linen-manufacturing towns. Kirkcaldy also became the centre of the Scottish linoleum industry. There was iron-smelting at several places in the area, most notably at the Carron ironworks near Falkirk. The Falkirk area also became one of the leading British centres for the manufacture of light iron castings, and West Lothian developed an extraordinary shale oil industry, based on locally mined shale, which supplied paraffin for lighting, wax for candles and lubricating oils for

Fig. 21. Methil Parish Church, Fife

Fig. 22. Our Lady, Star of the Sea Roman Catholic Church, Tayport, Fife

machinery. The employment created by this industrial expansion, and the fortunes made by entrepreneurs, resulted in the building of many fine churches in the areas affected. Some of these have been mentioned above. Others include the Free churches of St Brycedale, Kirkcaldy (**39**, 1877-81), Dunipace (1888-90); the United Presbyterian churches of Viewfield, Stirling (**94**, 1859-60), Broxburn (now parish, 1880) and Dundas, Grangemouth (1894); the Roman Catholic churches of St John Cantius and St Nicholas, Broxburn (1880, 1890), St Margaret's, Dunfermline (**52**, 1889), and the rebuilding of St Mary's, Bathgate (1908). Scottish Episcopal churches were usually smaller than those of the other major denominations, but often beautifully designed. Those in industrial towns included Christ's Church, Falkirk (1863-4), St John the Evangelist, Alloa (**61**, 1867-9) and Holy Trinity, Dunfermline (1891). Another exceptional Episcopal church of this period is Holy Trinity, Stirling (**89**, 1875-8).

There was a remarkable boom in church building in the late 1890s, and this was probably a contributory factor in the decision in 1900 by the Free and United Presbyterian churches to unite as the United Presbyterian Church. Between then and 1914, the new church built a number of new buildings in the area. These included Denny Westpark and St James's Falkirk, both started before the union, and completed in 1900, and Larbert East, St Andrew's Kirkcaldy (1902-3) and St Andrew's, Bo'ness (**95**, 1904-6). Erskine United Free Church, Burntisland (1900-3, Fig. 18) is still used by the denomination. The Church of Scotland added St Leonard's, St Andrews (1902-4, Fig. 19), St Serf's Tullibody (**67**, 1904) and Zetland, Grangemouth (**104**, 1910-11) and restored the medieval Holy Trinity,

Fig. 23. St Andrew's Roman Catholic Church, Livingston, West Lothian

St Andrew's (**20**, 1907–9) as well as other buildings mentioned above. Other early twentieth-century buildings included Episcopal churches at Inverkeithing (St Peter's, **56**, 1903–10), Burntisland (St Serf's, **32**, 1905) St Andrews (All Saints, **21**, 1907–9 and later), and Roman Catholic churches at

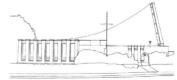

Fig. 24. Stirling North Parish Church

Stirling (St Mary's, **92**, 1904–5) and St Andrews (St James's, 1909–10). St Mary's, Bathgate (Fig. 20) was enlarged at about the same time.

The First World War effectively stopped church building, apart from the completion of a few planned before the war, but afterwards it resumed on a much less ambitious scale. Depression in most industries, emigration and migration to other parts of the United Kingdom, and falling earnings and profits were all contributory factors. The Roman Catholic and Scottish Episcopal churches were particularly active in building small churches, especially in mining areas, as the Fife and Lothian coalfields were developed to replace declining mining areas in the west of Scotland. Between 1920 and 1930 twelve Roman Catholic churches were built, the most interesting of which was Our Lady and St Ninian's, Bannockburn (**71**, 1927), a tall narrow church built largely of yellow brick. A few Episcopal churches were constructed, including the tiny, exotically Byzantine St Peter's, Linlithgow (**115**, 1928). During the same period, one Church of Scotland church, Methil (1924–5, Fig. 21), was constructed, and one United Free, Martyrs, St Andrews (**23**, 1926–8). Between 1924 and 1928, Kippen Parish Church (**84**) was remodelled on Scoto-Catholic lines, with many art works. Another fine church of the period was the Romanesque Bangour Hospital Chapel (1924–30). Economic pressure on the Presbyterian churches, however, grew to the extent that in 1929 the United Free Church and the Church of Scotland came together as the

Fig. 25. The former St Margaret's Anglican Church, Rosyth, Fife

Fig. 26. St Margaret's Parish Church, Glenrothes, Fife

Church of Scotland. The major reason for earlier splits – patronage – had by that time gone (in 1874). Some groups of United Free worshippers did not accept the union, and either retained their buildings, as in Burntisland and Dysart, or built new, small ones, as at Sauchie and Fishcross (1931–2) and at St Ninian's, Stirling (1934). The finest churches of the 1930s were probably those designed by Reginald Fairlie for the Roman Catholic church at Dunblane (The Holy Family, **79**, 1935), and Tayport (Our Lady, Star of the Sea, 1938–9, Fig. 22) On the whole, though, economic conditions in the area did not greatly improve before the Second World War again brought a stop to church building.

After the war, however, the coal-mining industry was revived by its nationalisation. The 'New Town' of Glenrothes was created to serve a new 'super-pit' and older pits in the central Forth Valley were modernised, with new housing areas created to serve them. Programmes of public housing round the major towns were also undertaken to allow substandard housing to be cleared. To cope with the closure of the West Lothian shale-oil industry a second 'New Town' was built, absorbing the sites of several shale-oil villages. All of this new housing called for new churches, and there was a boom in church building that lasted from the early 1950s to the early 1970s. Many of the churches constructed in this period were very basic structures, but there were some exceptional modern ones, notably St Paul's Roman Catholic Church (**35**, 1957–8) and St Columba's Church of Scotland (**33**, 1960–1), both in Glenrothes, St Andrew's Roman Catholic Church in Livingston (1959, Fig. 23), Brucefield Church of Scotland, Whitburn (1964) and Stirling North (1970–1, Fig. 24). Other interesting modern buildings are the circular St Columba's Roman Catholic Church, Cupar (1964), St Margaret's Anglican Church, Rosyth (1968–9, no longer a church, Fig. 25), and St Peter and St Paul's Roman

Fig. 27. St Ninian's Parish Church, Dunfermline, Fife

Catholic Church, also at Rosyth. The latter two churches were built for personnel at the naval base, which has now closed. There were also a few intentionally traditional churches built after the war, of which Deans, Livingston (1949), St Margaret's, Glenrothes (1953-4, Fig. 26) and The Holy Name Roman Catholic Church, Oakley (**57**, 1958) are the best. In recent years, west Fife and parts of West Lothian have become essentially dormitory suburbs of Edinburgh, and a few new churches have been built, including new Church of Scotland churches in Dunfermline and Dalgety Bay (**49**, 1980-1). Other new churches in the area have replaced postwar churches that did not wear well, notably in Bo'ness (St Mary of the Assumption, 1990) and Dunfermline (St Ninian's, 1997, Fig. 27), and some new buildings have been constructed by 'minority' churches, including Falkirk Free Church (**101**, 1998) and a Baptist church in Larbert (2000).

The rich and complex history of this part of Scotland is amply reflected in its heritage of churches, great and small, famous and little known. Many of them are members of Scotland's Churches Scheme, but it has not been possible to mention them all in this Introduction, which has been written to provide an overview. All these places of worship have something to say to us about change and continuity, about diversity of belief, but above all about the continuing vitality of Christianity in this area over many centuries.

Professor John R. Hume
Universities of Glasgow and St Andrews

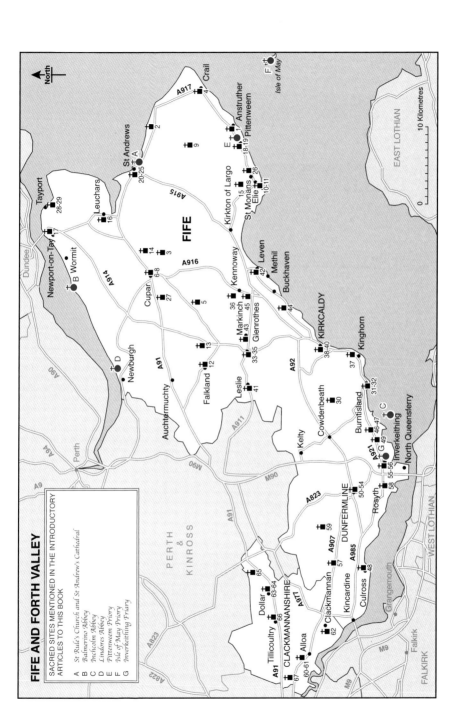

FIFE AND FORTH VALLEY

SACRED SITES MENTIONED IN THE INTRODUCTORY
ARTICLES TO THIS BOOK

A St Rule's Church and St Andrew's Cathedral
B Balmerino Abbey
C Inchcolm Abbey
D Lindores Abbey
E Pittenweem Priory
F Isle of May Priory
G Inverkeithing Friary

North

0   10 Kilometres

FIFE

PERTH
&
KINROSS

CLACKMANNANSHIRE

WEST LOTHIAN

EAST LOTHIAN

FALKIRK

Dundee

Perth

Tayport
Newport-on-Tay
B Wormit

Leuchars
16
17
D Newburgh
Auchtermuchty
Cupar
6-8
27
14
3

St Andrews
A
20-25
2
9

A917
Crail
4
Anstruther
Pittenweem
E
18-19
Isle of May
F

Kirkton of Largo
15
St Monans
Elie
26
10-11

A915

A916

Kennoway
Leven
Methil
Buckhaven
42
44

Falkland
Leslie
41
12
13

Markinch
Glenrothes
33-35
36
43
45
5

KIRKCALDY
38-40

Kinghorn
37

Cowdenbeath
30
Burntisland
31-32
C
North Queensferry
Inverkeithing
G
46-47
49
55-56
58
Rosyth
50-54
48

Kelty

DUNFERMLINE
A823

A907
A985
57
59

Kincardine
Culross

Clackmannan
62

Alloa
60-61
67

Tillicoultry
66
Dollar
65
63-64

A91

Grangemouth

Falkirk

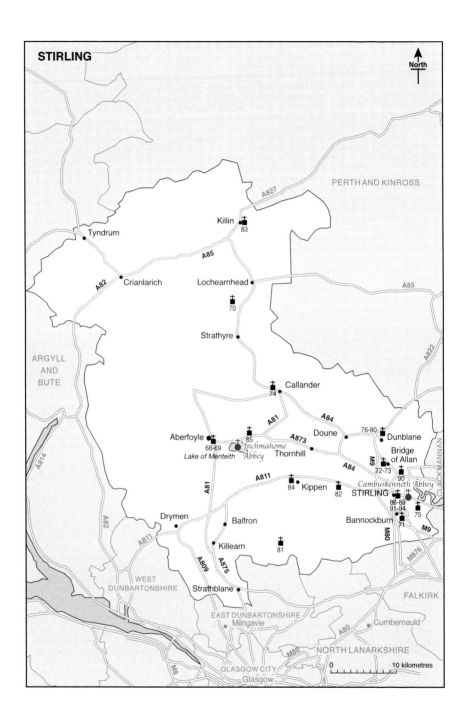

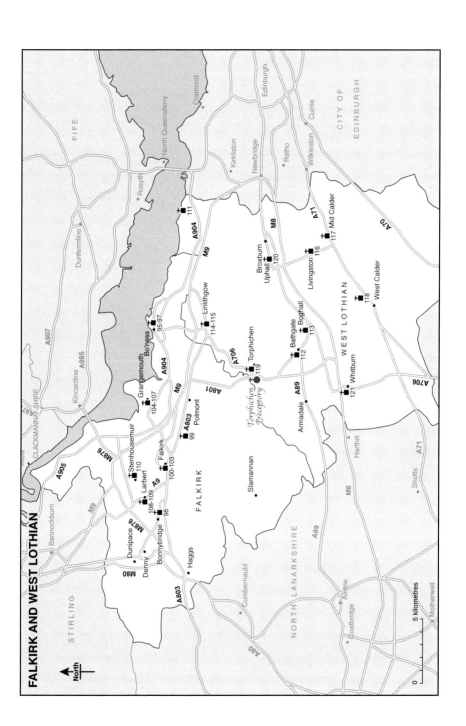

FALKIRK AND WEST LOTHIAN

North

FIFE

CITY OF EDINBURGH

Cramond

North Queensferry

Kirkliston

Newbridge

Ratho

Currie

Edinburgh

Wilkieston

Rosyth

Dunfermline

Kincardine

A907

A985

M9

A904

111

M9

A904

95-97

Bo'ness

Grangemouth

104-107

A803

Polmont

99

A9

Falkirk

100-103

Stenhousemuir

110

Larbert

108-109

98

FALKIRK

Linlithgow

114-115

Torphichen

A706

Torphichen

119

Torphichen
Preceptory

A801

Slamannan

Dunipace

Denny

Bonnybridge

Haggs

A803

M80

M876

M876

A9

A905

Alva

CLACKMANNANSHIRE

Bannockburn

STIRLING

M8

M8

Broxburn

Uphall

120

Livingston

116

A71

Mid Calder

117

118

West Calder

Bathgate

112

Boghall

113

Whitburn

121

A89

Armadale

A706

WEST LOTHIAN

A70

A71

Harthill

Shotts

NORTH LANARKSHIRE

A89

M8

Cumbernauld

A80

Airdrie

Coatbridge

Motherwell

5 kilometres

0

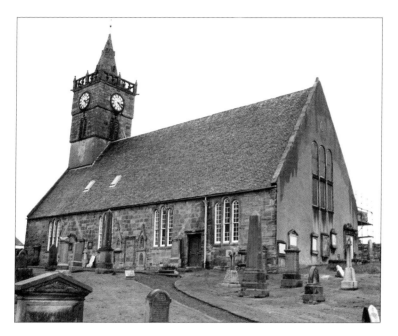

Anstruther Parish Church   1

All Saints', St Andrews   21

Church of the Holy Rude, Stirling   86

St John's Church, Alloa   61

Pittenweem Parish Church   18

St Athernase Parish Church,
Leuchars   16

St Athernase Parish Church, Leuchars   16

Balquhidder Old   70

Dunfermline Abbey   50

Aberfoyle Parish Church   68

Dunfermline Abbey   50

Torphichen Kirk   119

St Nicholas, Uphall   120

St Paul's Church, Glenrothes   35

Falkland Parish Church   12

Burntisland Parish Church   31

St James the Great, Dollar   64

Cults Kirk   5

Abercorn Kirk   111

Holy Trinity Church, Stirling   89

St Michael's Parish Church,
Linlithgow   114

Crail Parish Church   4

St Monans Parish Church   26

How to use this Guide

Entries are arranged by local authority area, with large areas sub-divided for convenience. The number preceding each entry refers to the map. Each entry is followed by symbols for access and facilities:

⚊	Ordnance Survey reference	👂	Hearing induction loop for the deaf
⚊	Denomination	👤	Welcomers and guides on duty
⊕	Church website	📖	Guidebooks and souvenirs available/for sale
●	Regular services		
○	Church events	(NADFAS)	Church Recorders' Inventory (NADFAS)
◐	Opening arrangements	👶	Features for children/link with schools
♿	Wheelchair access for partially abled	🍵	Refreshments
WC	Toilets available for visitors	Ⓐ	Category A listing
WC	Toilets adapted for the disabled available for visitors	Ⓑ	Category B listing
		Ⓒ	Category C listing

Category A: Buildings of national or international importance, either architectural or historic, or fine little-altered examples of some particular period, style or building type.

Category B: Buildings of regional or more than local importance, or major examples of some particular period, style or building type which may have been altered.

Category C: Buildings of local importance, lesser examples of any period, style, or building type, as originally constructed or moderately altered; and simple traditional buildings which group well with others in categories A and B.

The information appearing in the gazetteer of this guide is supplied by the participating churches. While this is believed to be correct at the time of going to press, Scotland's Churches Scheme cannot accept any responsibility for its accuracy.

❶ ANSTRUTHER PARISH CHURCH

St Adrian's Parish Church, Anstruther Easter
Burial Brae
Anstruther
KY10 3HF

NO 567 037
Church of Scotland

Off Crail Road.

James Melville (brother of Andrew, the leading Covenanter) inspired the purchase of land in 1590 for a new church, but he was exiled by James VI and the church was not built until 1634 and the tower 1644. The church with its round-headed windows and square tower was described in 1837 as 'one of the most elegant country churches anywhere to be seen'. Tahitian Princess buried outside the south wall. Many interesting features. Anstruther is the birthplace of Thomas Chalmers.

- Sunday: 11.00am; healing service 2nd Sunday of month, 2.00pm
- Open April to September: Tuesday 2.00–3.00pm, Thursday 11.00am–12.00 noon

❷ BOARHILLS CHURCH

Boarhills
KY16 8PW

NO 562 137
Church of Scotland

Linked with Martyrs St Andrews, Dunino

On A917 west of Boarhills.

The church was built 1866–7, although there has been a burial ground here considerably longer. The architect was George Rae. Original oil lamps, now converted to electricity.

- Sunday: 10.00am in February, April, June, August, October and December
- Open by arrangement (01334 880315)

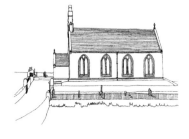

3 CERES PARISH CHURCH

**Kirk Brae
Ceres
KY15 5ND**

NO 399 117

Church of Scotland

Linked with Springfield, Kemback

Built 1806 to a design by Alexander Leslie, with a battlemented tower, its spire added in 1852. The building has the original box pews and long communion tables running the full length of the church. The 17th-century stone-slated Lindsay vault in the kirkyard was possibly attached to the medieval church.

- Sunday: 11.00am
- Open by arrangement (01334 828233)

4 CRAIL PARISH CHURCH

**Marketgate
Crail
KY10 3TU**

NO 613 080

Church of Scotland

www.crailchurch.org.uk

Consecrated 1243 with alterations 1526, 1796. Restored 1963. Judith Campbell windows (1970 and 1975). Pictish cross slab. 17th-century carving. Pipe organ by Harrison & Harrison 1892, rebuilt and installed here 1936. Graveyard (with dead house).

- Sunday: 11.15am; and 6.30pm June to August
- Open 2.00–4.00pm Tuesday, Wednesday and Thursday, June and August

5 CULTS KIRK

Kirkton of Cults
KY15 7TE

🅰 NO 347 099

⛪ Church of Scotland

🌐 www.friendsofcultskirk.org.uk

South side of A914, 0.8km (½ mile) from Pitlessie.

A place of worship since the 12th century, the present kirk built 1793. Bell inscribed 'John Meikle, Edinburgh, fecit for the Kirk of Cults, 1699'. Lepers window, Laird's Pew, memorials, one by Chantry of Sir David Wilkie RA, the most famous son of the Manse, one by Samuel Joseph of his father and mother. Wilkie Hall, Pitlessie village, collection of etchings and engravings by Wilkie, viewing by appointment (01337 830491).

- Sunday: 11.30am until September 2008, then 10.00am
- Open 8.00am–8.00pm

    (by arrangement)

6 CUPAR OLD & ST MICHAEL OF TARVIT PARISH CHURCH

Kirkgate
Cupar
KY15 5AL

🅰 NO 380 146

⛪ Church of Scotland

🌐 www.cuparoldparish.google pages.com

The tower dates from 1415; its spire and belfry (containing two bells 1485 and 1689) were added in 1620 and the four-face clock in 1910. The church itself was rebuilt in 1785. Inside are war memorials on the east and south walls and the guidon of the Fife and Forfar Yeomanry. A recess in the west wall contains the 15th-century recumbent figure of a knight ('Muckle Fernie'). Adjacent graveyard contains hand of David Hackston, a Covenanter from Rathillet.

- Sunday: September to May 11.00am; June to August 10.00am; September to May, Evening Service 6.30pm
- Open by arrangement (01334 655271)

7 ST JAMES THE GREAT, CUPAR

**St Catherine Street
Cupar
KY15 4HH**

⚔ NO 376 146

⛪ Scottish Episcopal

Simply detailed Gothic-style nave-and-chancel church built in 1866 to a design by Sir Robert Rowand Anderson. Fine choir screen, reredos and panelling by Sir Robert Lorimer, 1920. Organ originally by D. & T. Hamilton of Edinburgh 1875.

• Sunday: 8.00am and 11.00am; Wednesday: 10.00am
• Open weekdays, 10.00am–3.00pm

8 ST JOHN'S PARISH CHURCH, CUPAR

**77 Bonnygate
Cupar
KY15 4BY**

⚔ NO 373 147

⛪ Church of Scotland

🌐 www.cuparstjohns.org

The 46m (150ft) spire with belfry dominates the view of Cupar from the many approaches. Built 1878, Campbell Douglas & Sellars, Glasgow, when first Cupar Free Church became too small. Galleried interior. Set on a raised area in stepped gardens.

• Sunday: 11.15am; Wednesday 9.30am
• Open all year, Wednesday 9.30–11.30am, or by arrangement (01334 653258)

DUNINO CHURCH

**Dunino
KY16 8LU**

NO 541 109

Church of Scotland

Linked with Martyrs St Andrews, Boarhills

Off B9131, St Andrews–Anstruther road.

There has been a church at Dunino since 1240. The present exquisitely detailed building is of 1827 by James Gillespie Graham with the chancel and porch 1928 by J. Jeffrey Waddell & Young. Font by Sir Robert Lorimer, stained glass by J. Jennings of London and W. Wilson. Early Celtic carved stone in the churchyard.

- Sunday: 10.00am in January, March, May, July, September and November
- Open daily

10 ELIE PARISH CHURCH

**High Street
Elie
KY9 1DB**

NO 491 001

Church of Scotland

 www.eliekirk.co.uk

Linked with Kilconquhar

Originally erected in 1639. The tower was added in 1726 and the body of the kirk rebuilt 1831. The building is a typical T-plan post-Reformation kirk with the pulpit on the south wall. Opposite the pulpit is a laird's loft with the family vault beneath. 'Russell' stained glass windows either side of the pulpit and four further windows designed by Edward Burne-Jones.

- Sunday: 10.00am
- Open by arrangement (01333 330336)

11 ST MICHAEL & ALL ANGELS, ELIE

**Rotten Row
Elie
KY9 1AY**

A NO 484 001

 Scottish Episcopal

⊕ www.eastneuk-episcopal.co.uk/
st_michaels.html

Linked with St John's Pittenweem

Prefabricated wood-and-iron
structure, erected 1905 at Craigforth,
Earlsferry and moved to the present
site in 1924. Partly rebuilt after a fire
in 1954. Attractive interior, often
decorated with flowers. Carved stone
monuments to war dead (1920) and
founders (1936). Cousans chamber
organ acquired second-hand in 1976.

- Sunday: 9.45am
- Open by arrangement (01333 312555)

12 FALKLAND PARISH CHURCH

**The Square
Falkland
KY15 7DG**

A NO 252 074

 Church of Scotland

⊕ www.falkland-freuchie-churches.
org.uk

Linked with Freuchie

On the site of an earlier building,
the present church was completed
in 1850 to a design by David Bryce
and gifted to the people of Falkland
by Onesiphorus Tyndall Bruce, of
the family of Bruce of Earlshall. The
style is Victorian Gothic. Centre pews
convert to long communion tables.
Stained glass 1897. Organ by Hill,
Norman & Beard 1923.

- Sunday: 10.00am in even-numbered
years, 11.30am in odd-numbered
years
- Open mid-June to mid-September,
Monday to Friday 2.00–4.00pm, or
by arrangement (01337 857732)

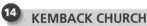

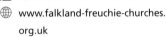

13 FREUCHIE PARISH CHURCH

**High Street
Freuchie
KY15 7EX**

― NO 284 067

― Church of Scotland

― www.falkland-freuchie-churches.
org.uk

Linked with Falkland

Simple Gothic style church of 1876 by Robert Baldie given dignity by a broach spire. Original furnishings. Stained glass by A. Ballantine & Co: three-light Transfiguration, single-light 'Suffer the Little Children …' and 'I am the Good Shepherd'. Wyvern electronic organ installed 1993.

- Sunday: 10.00am in odd-numbered years, 11.30am in even-numbered years
- Open by arrangement (01337 857432)

 (Wednesday 2.00–3.30pm)

14 KEMBACK CHURCH

**Kemback
KY15 5TS**

― NO 419 152

― Church of Scotland

― www.kemback.org

Linked with Ceres, Springfield

In centre of village, 4.8km (3 miles) east of Cupar.

The first church in the area was founded in 1244. In a document dated 1583 the Laird of Kemback granted a site for church, graveyard, manse and six acres of glebeland – this is the ruined church. The present simple church with Gothic details and bell-cote was built in 1814. The interior was renewed in 1920s using Borneo cedar. The bell is believed to come from the ruined church.

- Sunday: 9.45am
- Open by arrangement (01334 828233)

15 KILCONQUHAR PARISH CHURCH

**Main Street
Kilconquhar
KY9 1LF**

NO 485 020

Church of Scotland

www.eliekirk.co.uk

Linked with Elie

The church, with its prominent tower, stands on an elevated position between the road and Kilconquhar Loch. The ruins of an earlier church, dating from 1243, are to the east of the present building. The church, designed by R. & R. Dickson, is an exact copy of Cockpen Church in Midlothian, though in larger dimensions, by the same architect.

- Sunday: 11.30am, April to September
- Open during daylight hours during summer months

B

16 ST ATHERNASE PARISH CHURCH, LEUCHARS

**Main Street
Leuchars
KY16 0HD**

NO 455 214

Church of Scotland

www.leuchars.org.uk/StAthernase.php

Twelfth-century Norman church in a historic conservation setting. The chancel and apse with its two tiers of blind round-headed arcading and carved wallhead corbels is of outstanding architectural interest. Original masons' marks and carving can be found. The distinctive octagonal bell-tower was added in the 18th century and the nave in 1858 by John Milne. Restoration by Reginald Fairlie in 1914.

- Sunday: 11.00am
- Open April to October daily 9.30am–5.00pm, or by arrangement with Church Officer (01334 839709)

 (July and Aug, Tuesday 10.00am–12 noon and 2.00–4.00pm, or by arrangement)

(Tuesday 10.00am–4.00pm)

17 ST MARY'S EPISCOPAL CHURCH, NEWPORT

**10 High Street
Newport-on-Tay
DD6 8DA**

NO 420 278

Scottish Episcopal

Simple but picturesque church by architect T. M. Cappon, consecrated 1887. A plain interior, beautified from 1920 onwards with panelling, pulpit and windows – all donated as memorials. The rood screen of 1940 is by William Lamb. Organ 1903/4 by John Miller of Dundee, refurbished 2000 by Alex Edmonstone of Perth.

- Sunday: 10.45am
- Open by arrangement (01337 870294)

18 PITTENWEEM PARISH CHURCH

**Kirkgate
Pittenweem
KY10 2LF**

NO 549 026

Church of Scotland

This ancient monument has developed over a long time. The earliest work is around 1200. The church was extended in 1532 with an entrance from Cove Wynd, and the Tolbooth Tower and Bailies Loft were added in 1588. The interior was refurbished in 1883 in Victorian style with new entrance, galleries and stairs. The bell dates from 1662, while the clock in the tower is a fine example by John Smith. Stained glass by William Wilson and John Blyth of the 1950s and 1960s.

- Sunday: 11.30am
- Open weekdays 8.00am–6.00pm, keys from the Post Office (C. & A. Campbell's) in Market Place

19 ST JOHN THE EVANGELIST, PITTENWEEM

**Marygate
Pittenweem
KY10 2LH**

⚑ NO 550 026

🏠 Scottish Episcopal

🌐 www.eastneuk-episcopal.co.uk/
st_johns.html

Linked with St Michael Elie

Built 1805, enlarged 1869 and refurbished with carved wood panelling, pulpit and chancel furnishings by Robert Lorimer, 1925. Further improvements were made in 2001. Stained glass by Ballantine, 1879 and 1914. Chamber organ, probably by Renton, restored 1995.

- Sunday: 11.30am
- Open by arrangement (01333 312555)

20 PARISH CHURCH OF THE HOLY TRINITY, ST ANDREWS

**South Street
St Andrews
KY16 9UH**

⚑ NO 509 167

🏠 Church of Scotland

Tower and occasional pillars 1412, completely rebuilt on original ground plan in 1909, architect Peter MacGregor Chalmers. South porch commemorates John Knox preaching here. Much fine stained glass by Strachan, Davis, Hendrie, Wilson and others: clerestory windows have badges of all Scottish regiments of First World War. Elaborate memorial pulpit of Iona marble, alabaster and onyx. Decorated font of Caen stone. Memorial tomb of Archbishop Sharp. Oak barrel roof. Hunter Memorial Aisle has much fine wood-carving. 17th-century sacramental silver. Harrison & Harrison organ. Twenty-seven-bell Taylor of Loughborough carillon.

- Sunday: 11.00am
- Open Tuesday and Saturday 10.00am–12.00 noon, or by arrangement (01334 478317)

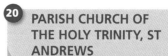

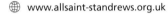

21 ALL SAINTS' CHURCH, ST ANDREWS

**North Castle Street
St Andrews
KY16 9BG**

NO 512 168

Scottish Episcopal

www.allsaint-standrews.org.uk

Complex of church hall, rectory and club in Scottish vernacular with an Italian flavour. Orange pantiled roofs and lots of crowsteps. Slated chancel and bell-tower by John Douglas of Chester 1906–9; the rest is by Paul Waterhouse 1919–24. Woodwork of rood, chapel altarpiece and front canopy by Nathaniel Hitch, stone Madonna and Child by Hew Lorimer 1945, marble font and wrought-iron screen by Farmer & Brindley. Three windows by Herbert Hendrie, Louis Davis and Douglas Strachan.

- Sunday: 8.00am, 10.00am and 6.00pm; Monday: 8.00am; Tuesday: 6.00pm; Wednesday, Friday, Saturday: 9.30am; Thursday: 12.15pm
- Open daily 10.00am–4.30pm

 (Ladyhead book and coffee shop)

22 HOPE PARK CHURCH, ST ANDREWS

**St Mary's Place
St Andrews
KY16 9UY**

NO 505 167

Church of Scotland

www.hopeparkchurch.co.uk

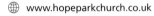

Opposite bus station.

Large Gothic church completed in 1865, by Peddie & Kinnear. The tower and spire are a landmark in the west end of the town. Rose windows with plate tracery in the broad transepts. Stained glass. Unusual canopy pulpit. Pewter communion ware, pulpit falls.

- Sunday: 9.30am and 11.00am
- Open Wednesday 10.00am–4.00pm July to August, also Holy Week and Christmas week, Monday to Friday 10.00am–4.00pm

23 MARTYRS CHURCH, ST ANDREWS

**North Street
St Andrews
KY16 9AH**

⚑ NO 510 168

⛪ Church of Scotland

Linked with Dunino, Boarhills

Opposite University Chapel.

Originally United Free Church, 1926–8 by Gillespie & Scott. Woodwork by Andrew Thom & Sons of St Andrews. Stained glass by Douglas Strachan, Herbert Hendrie, William Wilson, Sadie McLellan and Marjorie Kemp. Roll of Honour designed and painted by J. D. Macgregor.

• Sunday: 11.15am
• Open by arrangement (01334 474840)

  (side door)

24 ST ANDREW'S CHURCH, ST ANDREWS

**Queen's Terrace
St Andrews
KY16 9QF**

⚑ NO 509 164

⛪ Scottish Episcopal

🌐 www.st-andrews-church.net

Church in First-Pointed Early-English style by Sir Robert Rowand Anderson, 1869. Nave and chancel with narrow aisles separated from the nave by an arcade with leafy capitals. Fine 19th-century stained glass in the east and west walls. Two bays of excellent modern stained glass work. An open church policy and friendly welcome are a stable mission of this vibrant and enthusiastic congregation.

• Sunday: Holy Communion 8.00am and 10.00am, Choral Evensong 6.00pm; Monday to Friday: Morning Prayer 8.30am; Friday Holy Communion 11.00am
• Open 8.30am–5.00pm daily

25 ST SALVATOR'S, ST ANDREWS

**North Street
St Andrews
KY16 9AG**

Ⓐ NO 510 168

▥ Ecumenical

⊕ www.st-andrews.ac.uk/chaplaincy

Consecrated in 1460, the Church of St Salvator was established as an integral part of St Salvator's College, founded in 1450 by Bishop James Kennedy. Since 1904 it has been the official University Chapel. Refurnished by Reginald Fairlie from 1931. Notable features include Kennedy's tomb, a medieval Sacrament House, the 'John Knox' pulpit, the Communion table and First World War memorial with mosaics by Strachan. Hradetzky organ. Fine stained glass.

- Sunday (term-time only): 11.00am; Evensong: Wednesday 5.30pm (as advertised)
- Open 9.00am–5.00pm Monday to Friday

26 ST MONANS PARISH CHURCH

**Braehead
St Monans
KY10 2DB**

Ⓐ NO 523 014

▥ Church of Scotland

Occupying a striking position close to the sea, the church was built by Sir William Dishington 1370, with alterations by William Burn 1828 and Ian G. Lindsay 1961. 14th-century sedilia, piscina and aumbry. Medieval consecration crosses. Early 19th-century votive model ship of the line, heraldic bosses. Organ from Saughtonhall Congregational Church, Edinburgh, installed here 1995. External angled buttresses and 'buckle' corbels.

- Sunday: 10.00am
- Open April to October during daylight hours

27 SPRINGFIELD PARISH CHURCH

**Manse Road
Springfield
KY15 5RY**

NO 342 119

Church of Scotland

Linked with Ceres, Kemback

Built in 1861 to a plain, rectangular design with large round-headed windows and a corbelled birdcage bellcote with small obelisk. Light and airy interior with gallery. Notable late Victorian stained glass windows by Ballantine and Gardiner. The building was refurbished in 1970.

- Sunday: 9.45am
- Open by arrangement (01334 828233)

28 TAYPORT PARISH CHURCH

**Ferryport-on-Craig
Free Church
Queen Street
Tayport
DD6 9JZ**

NO 457 284

Church of Scotland

Opposite the War Memorial.

Built as Ferryport-on-Craig Free Church in 1843, united with Ferryport-on-Craig Parish Church and Erskine United Presbyterian Church in 1978. Stone Gothic-style hall church, the façade divided by buttresses with truncated finials and surmounted by an octagonal belfry with small slated spire.

- Sunday: 11.00am
- Open by arrangement (01382 552861)

FIFE

EAST

FIFE

EAST/CENTRAL

29 ST MARGARET OF SCOTLAND, TAYPORT

**Queen Street
Tayport
DD6 9JZ**

⚔ NO 467 284

⛪ Scottish Episcopal

A fine and unusual late-Victorian Gothic building of buttressed facing brick, with a vaulted timber interior. Designed by T. Martin Cappon and built in 1896. Its brick construction makes it unique among buildings of a similar date in Tayport, which are of stone, as are nearby examples of Cappon's work: St Mary's in Newport-on-Tay and the Leng Memorial Chapel at Vicarsford.

- Sunday: 10.30am
- Open by arrangement (01382 553701 or 01382 552272)

30 AUCHTERTOOL KIRK

**Auchtertool
KY2 5XW**

⚔ NT 208 902

⛪ Church of Scotland

🌐 www.auchtertoolkirk.org.uk

Linked with Linktown Kirkcaldy

1.6km (1 mile) west of Auchtertool village.

Pilgrims travelling between Inchcolm and St Andrews would stop at an ancient well and the panoramic view makes this still a special place. The earliest record of a church here is 1178; there are records for ministers from 1574. The present church was reconstructed in 1833 using earlier fabric. Stained glass includes a window of St Andrew used as inspiration for concerts. Many improvements, including the pipe organ by Casson & Millar, were the gift of one minister, the Rev. William Stevenson. A table gravestone in the churchyard is dated 1604.

- Sunday: 9.30am
- Open by arrangement (01592 781066)

31 BURNTISLAND PARISH CHURCH

**East Leven Street
Burntisland
KY3 9DX**

🅰 NT 234 857

⛪ Church of Scotland

🌐 www.burntislandkirk.org.uk

One of the first post-Reformation churches built in Scotland, still in use. Built in 1592 to an unusual square plan with a central tower. Semicircular arches link the four corner piers and give the centralised plan great dignity. The fronts of the four galleries and the Magistrates' Pew have painted panels of the late 16th and early 17th centuries. The General Assembly of the Church of Scotland met in Burntisland in May 1601 in the presence of James VI when a new translation of the Bible was approved. Organ originally by Cousans 1909. Extensive refurbishment completed in 1999.

- Sunday: 11.00am
- Open by arrangement (01592 873275)

 (by arrangement)

32 ST SERF'S, BURNTISLAND

**Ferguson Place
Burntisland
KY3 9ES**

🅰 NT 230 864

⛪ Scottish Episcopal

🌐 www.standrews.anglican.org

Linked with St Columba's Aberdour, St Peter's Inverkeithing

Junction with Cromwell Road.

Built in 1905 by W. R. Simpson from a design by Truro Cathedral architect J. L. Pearson. The stone is from the local Grange quarry. The chancel is divided from the nave by a fine Gothic arch. The east end of the chancel is semi-octagonal behind a triform arch springing from slender columns, surmounted by a Gothic arch. Stained glass by J. Powell & Sons, 1910.

- Sunday: 9.30am; Tuesday: 11.00am
- Open by arrangement (01592 873117)

33 ST COLUMBA'S, GLENROTHES

**Rothes Road
Glenrothes
KY6 1BN**

NO 270 009

Church of Scotland

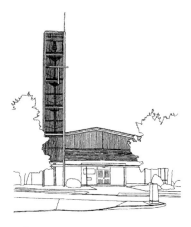

Built in 1960 and designed in conjunction with the theologians at St Mary's College of St Andrews University, with the emphasis on how the Scottish Reformation could be best expressed in a church building. The sanctuary features seating around three sides, with the Lord's table in the centre. Mural by Alberto Morrocco measuring 18m × 2.7m (59ft × 9ft) of scenes from the last days of Christ. Iron bell-tower is a landmark in the centre of the town.

* Sunday: 11.00am September to June; 10.00am July to August
* Open by arrangement (01592 754320)

34 ST LUKE THE EVANGELIST, GLENROTHES

**Ninian Quadrant
Glenrothes
KY7 4HP**

NO 273 008

Scottish Episcopal

By J. Cassells 1960, the church is a modern interpretation of the Perpendicular style, set alongside a playpark in the earliest and most central part of the new town of Glenrothes. Furnished with the warmth of pine, its interior is light and airy with an unusual layout, and houses several items of interest.

* Sunday: 9.30am and 11.00am
* Open Monday and Thursday 10.00am–1.00pm, Tuesday 9.00–10.30am, Sunday 9.15am–1.00pm

35 ST PAUL'S CHURCH, GLENROTHES

**Warout Road
Glenrothes
KY7 4ER**

NO 281 005

Roman Catholic

www.stpaulsandstmarys.co.uk

Linked with St Mary Leslie

Corner of Woodside Road/Warout Road.

Completed 1957 from design by Isi Metzstein and Andy McMillan of Gillespie, Kidd & Coia. Described by *The Scotsman* as 'the most significant piece of architecture north of the English Channel' and in *The Twentieth Century Church* as 'a homage to architecture's liberating function'. Interior contains the *Catalonian* altar crucifix 1957 and *The Madonna* or *Lady Piece* by Benno Schotz 1960. Carved Stations of the Cross and figure of St Paul by Harry Bain 1983.

- Sunday: 11.30am
- Open 1st Saturday of the month, 11.00am–6.00pm

36 ST KENNETH'S PARISH CHURCH, KENNOWAY

**Cupar Road
Kennoway
KY8 5LR**

NO 350 023

Church of Scotland

www.st-kenneths.freeserve.co.uk

Linked with Windygates

The church in Kennoway dates back to St Kenneth, who preached in the 6th century. The present Romanesque-style church with nave, aisles and tower was built in 1850 and was designed by Thomas Hamilton. Galleried interior. Six stained glass windows by Marjorie Kemp 1950. Monuments to past ministers.

- Sunday: 11.15am and, during term-time, 7.00pm
- Open by arrangement (01333 351372)

37 KINGHORN PARISH CHURCH

**St James Place
Kinghorn
KY3 9SU**

Ⓐ NT 272 869

🏛 Church of Scotland

The Kirk by the Sea for over 750 years has an unrivalled view across the beach to the Firth of Forth and Edinburgh. It has a historic bell-tower and a 'Sailors' Aisle' built in 1609 celebrating the naval connection and a model of the first Unicorn.

• Sunday: 9.30am and 11.00am (except 1st Sunday of month – 10.30am in church hall)
• Open every Tuesday 6.00–8.00pm

38 ST BRYCE KIRK (OLD KIRK), KIRKCALDY

**Old Parish Church
Kirk Wynd
Kirkcaldy
KY1 1EH**

Ⓐ NT 280 917

🏛 Church of Scotland

🌐 www.stbrycekirk.org

Linked with St Brycedale

Consecrated in 1244 by the Bishop of St Andrews, the ancient tower offers excellent views of Kirkcaldy. The body of the church is by James Elliot 1808, remodelled in 1987. Good stained glass windows, some by Morris & Co from Burne-Jones designs of 1886. Historic graveyard.

• Sunday: 11.00am, alternate Sundays
• Open by arrangement (01592 640016)

39 ST BRYCE KIRK (ST BRYCEDALE), KIRKCALDY

St Brycedale
St Brycedale Avenue
Kirkcaldy
KY1 1ET

NT 279 917

Church of Scotland

www.stbrycekirk.org

Linked with St Bryce

Junction with Kirk Wynd.

Built as a Free Church 1877–81 by James Matthews of Aberdeen. A 60m (197ft) tower and spire and associated pyramid-roofed twin towers lift the church out of the ordinary. In 1988 a transformed church at first-floor level was created above a multipurpose ground floor. Organ by Brindley & Foster 1893. Stained glass includes windows by Adam & Small 1881, Douglas Strachan 1923, and Edward Burne-Jones (executed by William Morris & Co) 1889.

- Sunday: 11.00am, alternate Sundays
- Open Monday to Thursday 9.00am–10.00pm, Friday 9.00am–3.00pm

40 LINKTOWN CHURCH, KIRKCALDY

Bethelfield Church
Bethelfield Place
Nicol Street
Kirkcaldy
KY1 2TJ

NT 278 910

Church of Scotland

www.linktown.org.uk

Linked with Auchtertool

With a parish covering most of the south of Kirkcaldy, Linktown is a buzzing church, hosting activities for all. A classical Secession church, by George Hay, 1831, its gable is decorated with urns. Fine interior with a horseshoe gallery supported on cast-iron Corinthian columns. Halls added 1897.

- Sunday: 11.00am
- Open by arrangement (01592 641080)

FIFE

CENTRAL

41 ST MARY, MOTHER OF GOD, LESLIE

Leslie Free Church
High Street
Leslie
KY6 3DJ

⚔ NO 251 018

⛪ Roman Catholic

🌐 www.stpaulsandstmarys.co.uk

Linked with St Paul's Glenrothes

Gothic church with 37m (120ft) spire by R. Thornton Shiells 1879. Originally Leslie Free Church, it was opened as Roman Catholic in 1959. Devastated by fire in 2004, the church has been restored by the efforts of the congregation, the architect for the restoration being Gray, Marshall & Associates. During the restoration, more light was brought in by opening up the five-light window behind the altar with windows by Lorraine Lamond.

• Saturday Vigil: 6.00pm; Tuesday and Thursday: 10.00am
• Open by arrangement (01592 752543)

42 LEVEN PARISH CHURCH

Scoonie Kirk
Durie Street
Leven
KY8 4HA

⚔ NO 383 017

⛪ Church of Scotland

🌐 www.levenparish.org.uk

Scoonie Kirk is the original Parish Church of Leven with its roots going back over sixteen centuries. The church moved to its present site in 1775. In 1904 the building was rebuilt and enlarged to a design by the eminent church architect Peter MacGregor Chalmers which incorporated some of the earlier building. The unique pipe organ was built by the French organ builder August Gern 1884 and was restored 1992. The building also has some very striking stained glass windows.

• Sunday: 11.00am
• Open Easter to September, Tuesday 11.00am–1.00pm, or by arrangement (01333 423969)

43 MARKINCH PARISH CHURCH

St Drostan
Kirk Brae
Markinch
KY7 6DS

 NO 297 019

Church of Scotland

www.markinchchurch.org.uk

Originally named St Drostan, after the 6th-century missionary. Records show the site has been a place of worship for almost 1,500 years. The Norman tower is 12th century; the body of the church was built 1768–88 and designed by Thomas and George Barclay. Session house by E. Robert Hutchison 1839. Organ chamber by Gillespie & Scott 1913. Clock of 1839.

- Sunday: 11.00am
- Open June to August, Tuesday and Thursday 1.30–4.30pm, Saturday 10.00am–4.30pm

44 THE CHURCH AT WEST WEMYSS

Main Street
West Wemyss
KY1 4SP

NT 328 949

Church of Scotland

Built in 1890, Alexander Tod, simple crow-stepped cruciform church of pink sandstone. Spiral tracery in the gable's big rose window. Repurchased from the Church of Scotland in 1972 by Captain Michael Wemyss, who agreed to maintain the building externally if the church continued to be used for worship. The congregation of Wemyss Parish Church is responsible for the interior and continuing worship. Beautiful mural by William McLaren on the inner wall of the transept which now accommodates halls, vestry and kitchen. New wall hangings 2001, sewn by members on the theme 'Jesus, Light of the World'. Old graveyard.

- Sunday: 10.00am
- Open by arrangement (01592 651498)

 (by arrangement)

45 ST KENNETH'S PARISH CHURCH, WINDYGATES

**The Cross
Windygates
KY8 5DD**

A NO 346 006

♁ Church of Scotland

⊕ www.st-kenneths.freeserve.co.uk

Linked with St Kenneth's Kennoway

Originally the United Free Church built by James McIntosh in 1926. Simple rectangular church with Gothic details. Inside, the original pews, boarded timber and open-beam ceiling and boarded timber dado survive.

- Sunday: 9.45am
- Open by arrangement (01333 351372)

46 ST COLUMBA'S, ABERDOUR

**Inverkeithing Road
Aberdour
KY3 0RS**

A NT 186 851

♁ Scottish Episcopal

⊕ www.standrews.anglican.org

Linked with St Serf's Burntisland, St Peter's Inverkeithing

Built in 1843 for the Earl of Moray as a private chapel for his employees in Aberdour. It was transferred to the Scottish Episcopal Church in 1918. A cruciform plan, tall and light with lancet windows. The west window blocked off by the addition of a balcony, which has recently been enclosed.

- Sunday: 11.00am
- Open by arrangement (01383 860521 or 01383 860795)

47 ST FILLAN'S, ABERDOUR

**Hawkcraig Road
Aberdour
KY3 0UP**

⟂ NT 193 855

⛪ Church of Scotland

🌐 www.stfillans.presbytery.org.uk

One of the finest examples of
Norman architecture in Scotland,
this 'miniature Cathedral' sits in its
own graveyard overlooking Aberdour
harbour. The early church, standing
in 1123, consisted of the nave and
chancel, lit by deep splayed windows
which still exist. The church was
enlarged in the 15th century by the
addition of a side aisle, and in the
17th by the small transeptual aisle,
now used by the choir. The church fell
into disrepair in the 18th century and
was restored in 1925. 'Even to enter St
Fillan's is to worship.'

- Sunday: 10.30am
- Flower Festival 1st week of August
- Open daily during daylight hours

48 CULROSS ABBEY

**Kirk Street
Culross
KY12 8JB**

⟂ NS 988 863

⛪ Church of Scotland

🌐 www.culrossandtorryburn
church.org

Built on the site of a Celtic Christian
Culdee church. Abbey founded in 1217
by Malcolm, 7th Earl of Fife; dedicated
to St Mary and St Serf. Much of the
original building remains, although a
great deal of it is in ruins. The monks'
choir forms the present parish
church, in continuous use since 1633.
Modernised in 1824 and restored in
1905 by Sir Robert Rowand Anderson.
Many features of interest.

- Sunday: 11.30am
- Open daily, summer 10.00am–dusk,
  winter 10.00am–4.00pm

FIFE

WEST

 49 DALGETY PARISH CHURCH

**Regents Way
Dalgety Bay
KY11 9UY**

🏛 NT 155 836
⛪ Church of Scotland
🌐 www.dalgety-church.co.uk

A hall church designed by Marcus Johnston, built in 1981 and extended in 1991. Worship area and suite of halls which are used by congregation and local community groups. War memorial in grounds.

- Sunday: 9.30am and 11.00am except last Sunday of the month: 10am
- Open by arrangement with church office (01383 824092)

50 DUNFERMLINE ABBEY

**St Margaret Street
Dunfermline
KY12 7PH**

🏛 NT 090 873
⛪ Church of Scotland
🌐 www.dunfermlineabbey.co.uk

Founded in 1072. Consists today of the nave of medieval monastic church (1150) and the modern parish church (1821) erected over foundations of original Choir. Burial place of King Robert the Bruce and numerous other Scottish royals including Malcolm III (Canmore) and his Queen, St Margaret of Scotland. Exquisitely carved pulpit by William Paterson, Edinburgh 1890. Fine pipe organ of 1882, rebuilt Walker in 1966.

- Sunday: 9.30am and 11.00am
- Open April to October, Monday to Saturday 10.00am–4.30pm, and Sunday 2.00–4.30pm, or by arrangement (01383 735182)

51 ST LEONARD'S, DUNFERMLINE

**2 Brucefield Avenue
Dunfermline
KY12 4SX**

NT 096 869

Church of Scotland

www.stleonardsparishchurch.org.uk

The most striking feature of the church, Peter MacGregor Chalmers 1904, is a round Celtic tower. Inside, the semicircular apse has a dramatic painting of the Risen Christ surrounded by Gospel characters, designed by the architect and painted by Mr A. Samuel 1927. Heraldic gallery dedicated to the Scottish Wars of Independence led by Wallace and Bruce.

- Sunday: June to August 10.00am; September to May 9.30am and 11.00am
- Open Tuesday and Thursday mornings (enter through church office)

52 ST MARGARET'S MEMORIAL CHURCH, DUNFERMLINE

**Holyrood Place
Dunfermline
KY12 7HZ**

NT 096 876

Roman Catholic

www.stmargaretsdunfermline.co.uk

A commanding building forming part of the ancient gateway to the town at the East Port. Designed in 1889 by Sir Robert Rowand Anderson in 12th-century Transitional style and completed in 1896. Stained glass circular window by John Blyth, stone reredos by Hew Lorimer, wood carving by Steven Foster and historical prints by Jurek Pütter. Three new stained glass windows by Douglas Hogg.

- Saturday: 6.30pm; Sunday: 9.00am and 11.00am; Weekdays: 10.00am
- Open by arrangement (01383 625611)

VIEWFIELD BAPTIST CHURCH, DUNFERMLINE

**East Port
Dunfermline
KY12 7HZ**

NT 095 875

Baptist

www.viewfield.org.uk

Gothic design by Peter L. Henderson, 1882–4. Front façade skewed giving a vestibule narrower at one side than the other and making necessary the cylindrical addition for the east gallery staircase. Wood vaulted ceiling upheld by laminated wood arches, supported internally by six cast-iron pillars. Pipe organ.

- Sunday: 11.00am and 6.30pm
- Open by arrangement with church office (01383 620465) 9.30am–2.30pm

   (Viewfield Centre, 10.00am–1200 noon, Mon to Fri)

 ST ANDREW'S ERSKINE CHURCH, DUNFERMLINE

**1–3 Lorimer Gardens
Dunfermline
KY12 0BJ**

NT 107 886

Church of Scotland

Junction with Robertson Road.

New church, built in 2004, and designed by Dearle & Henderson. Constructed of red brick with a white rendered wall to the road, the advanced central section bearing a large incised cross. Dramatic curved metal roof and clerestory windows.

- Sunday: 10.30am
- Open Tuesday 9.30am–12.30pm, Thursday and Friday 9.30am–2.00pm during school term, 9.30–11.30am outwith school term

FIFE

WEST

55 INVERKEITHING PARISH CHURCH

St Peter's
Church Street
Inverkeithing
KY11 1LQ

 NT 131 830

Church of Scotland

A Norman foundation, church dedicated to St Peter 1244. The present building is a nave and aisles church by Gillespie Graham 1827 attached to a 14th-century tower. Refurbished 1900, Peter MacGregor Chalmers. Fourteenth-century stone font, one of the finest in Scotland, thought to have been gifted by Robert III for the baptism of his son the Duke of Rothesay. Ongoing refurbishment, access may be restricted.

- Sunday: 11.30am
- Open July to August, Saturday 10.00am–12.00 noon
- Open by arrangement (01383 413399)

56 ST PETER'S EPISCOPAL CHURCH, INVERKEITHING

Hope Street
Inverkeithing
KY11 1LW

 NT 128 827

Scottish Episcopal

www.inverkeithingepiscopal.org.uk

Linked with St Serf's Burntisland, St Columba's Aberdour

The church was built to serve the Scottish Episcopal community in Jamestown, at one time outside the Royal Burgh of Inverkeithing. The nave was built in 1903 to a design by Henry F. Kerr and the chancel added in 1910. The interior was altered in 1980 to form a worship area and hall. Set in well-kept gardens on the southern approach to the town from the Forth Road Bridge.

- Sunday: Holy Communion 11.00am
- Open by arrangement (01383 414194)

57 CHURCH OF THE HOLY NAME, OAKLEY

**Station Road
Oakley
KY12 9NW**

Ⓐ NT 025 885
🏛 Roman Catholic

Built by the Smith-Sligo family of Inzievar House to a 1958 design by Charles W. Gray. Consecrated October 1965. Outstanding features include stained glass windows by Gabriel Loire of Chartres. Carved Stations of the Cross also by Gabriel Loire.

- Saturday Vigil: 6.30pm; Sunday Mass: 10.15am
- Open by arrangement (01383 850335)

 Ⓑ

58 ROSYTH METHODIST CHURCH

**Queensferry Road
Rosyth
KY11 2JH**

Ⓐ NT 114 842
🏛 Methodist/Scottish Episcopal

Junction with Woodside Avenue.

Founded in 1916, the present building was opened in 1970. A sanctuary of A-frame design with single-storey hall and ancillary rooms adjoining by Alan Mercer, architect. Striking 9m (30ft) high mural, painted in Byzantine style by Derek Seymour.

- Sunday: 9.30am (Scottish Episcopal), 11.00am (Methodist)
- Open by arrangement (01383 415458)

59 SALINE CHURCH

Blairingone
Main Street
Saline
KY12 9TL

NT 023 923

Church of Scotland

Typical church of the early 19th century, 1810 by William Stark. Session house added 1819 and hall in 1972. Stained glass in the east window depicting Christ with the symbols of Baptism and the Eucharist by John Blyth, 1984. A number of old records and photos are available.

- Sunday: 10.30am
- Open Wednesday 2.00–4.00pm May to beginning of September, or by arrangement (01383 852209 or 01383 852730)

 (by arrangement)

60 ALLOA PARISH CHURCH (ST MUNGO'S)

Bedford Place
Alloa
FK10 1LJ

NS 886 929

Church of Scotland

Delicate and picturesque Gothic Revival church by James Gillespie Graham 1816–19. Usual symmetry in plan, but greater felicity than normal in lacy Perpendicular. The 63m (207ft_ spire with flying buttresses is visible from most parts of the town. Interior is by Leslie Grahame MacDougall in Lorimer-derived Gothic.

- Sunday: 11.15am
- Open by arrangement (01259 214494)

61 ST JOHN'S CHURCH, ALLOA

Broad Street
Alloa
FK10 1AN

⛰ NS 886 925

⛪ Scottish Episcopal

🌐 www.stjohnsalloa.org.ok

Sir Robert Rowand Anderson designed St John's which was opened in 1869 and enlarged in 1873. Described by Thomas Bradshaw then as the 'most elegant place of worship in the County'. Early Geometric Gothic with a notable broach spire. The rich interior includes glass by Kempe, and a reredos with a mosaic of the Last Supper by the Italian Salviatti. The chancel was refurbished in 1913, its roof bearing 106 carved bosses. These, together with the woodwork of the choirstalls 1902, organ screen and war memorial, are all by Lorimer. The tower contains a ring of eight bells, six hung in 1871 and a further two in 1925.

- Sunday: 10.30am
- Open usually Wednesday and Friday 10.00am–12.30pm, or by arrangement (01259 212836)

62 CLACKMANNAN PARISH CHURCH

High Street
Clackmannan
FK10 4JG

⛰ NS 910 918

⛪ Church of Scotland

🌐 www.clackmannankirk.org

There has been a church at Clackmannan since St Serf visited from Culross in the 8th century. The present church was built in 1815 by James Gillespie Graham to replace a 13th-century church. Perpendicular Gothic with buttressed tower at the west end. Stained glass by Herbert Hendrie, Gordon Webster, Sadie Pritchard and Douglas Hamilton. Modern Makin Toccata digital computerised organ. Graveyard has stones dating from the 17th century with several Bruce family memorials. Views over Carse of Forth.

- Sunday: 11.00am September to June, 10.30am July and August
- Open weekdays 2.00–4.00pm mid-June to mid-September, or by arrangement (01259 214238 or 01259 211255)

CLACKMANNAN

63 DOLLAR PARISH CHURCH

**East Burnside
Dollar
FK14 7AJ**

⚑ NS 964 980

⛪ Church of Scotland

🌐 www.dollarparishchurch.org.uk

Linked with Muckhart

Built 1842–3 to replace 18th-century church (ruin to north), designed by Tite of London. Chancel added 1926, porch added 1963. Triple stained glass window in memory of Rev. Angus Gunn 1910. Three stained glass windows by Adam Robson and Jennifer Campbell, Union window 1979 by Douglas Hogg. Millennium glass screens designed by Angus Maclean 2003. Rushworth and Dreaper organ 1926. Reredos tapestry based on Ardchattan Cross designed by Adam Robson 1963.

- Sunday: 11.15am
- Open by arrangement (01259 743432)

64 ST JAMES THE GREAT, DOLLAR

**Harviestoun Road
Dollar
FK14 7HF**

⚑ NS 958 980

⛪ Scottish Episcopal

A small country church with a prayerful atmosphere, set in a well-kept garden. Consecrated in 1882, the building was designed by Thomas Frame & Son, Alloa. The font is a memorial to Archbishop Archibald Campbell Tait of Canterbury (1868–83).

- Sunday: 8.30am and 10.30am and (3rd Sunday) 6.30pm; Thursday: 9.45am
- Open daily during daylight hours

65 MUCKHART PARISH CHURCH

8 Kirk Hill
Pool of Muckhart
FK14 7JQ

⚐ NO 001 010

 Church of Scotland

Linked with Dollar

North side of A91 .

Typical Georgian church of 1838 although four skewputts are dated 1620, 1699, 1713 and 1789. Rectangular in plan with small bellcote on the west gable. Stained glass windows removed to Fossoway Church, Crook of Devon. Various plaques. Large grave stone on east wall of the church for the Christie family, Cowden. Nearby stone to Matsui, Japanese gardener to Miss Ella Christie.

- Sunday: 9.45am
- Open daily

66 TILLICOULTRY PARISH CHURCH

17 Dollar Road
Tillicoultry
FK13 6PD

⚐ NS 923 968

🏠 Church of Scotland

🌐 www.tillicoultryparishchurch
org.uk

South side of A91.

Neo-Perpendicular, rectangular church by William Stirling of Dunblane 1829. Central gable topped with corbelled-out octagonal belfry. The original horseshoe gallery was replaced with a single gallery in 1920. Stained glass window of 1924 in memory of the Rev. Joseph Conn. Three-light window by Douglas Strachan featuring the Crucifixion, Joseph, and David instructing Solomon.

- Sunday: 9.00am and 10.30am, evening service 6.30pm (last Sunday of month)
- Open Thursday, June to August 2.00–4.00pm, or by arrangement (01259 750927)

67 ST SERF'S PARISH CHURCH, TULLIBODY

**16 Menstrie Road
Tullibody
FK10 2RG**

A NS 860 954

Church of Scotland

Charmingly simple Norman-style church of 1904 by Peter MacGregor Chalmers. Nave and side aisles separated by five pillared arches, apse and transepts and an open dressed-timber roof. Stained glass by Stephen Adam, Norman M. McDougall. Nearby ruins of the former church.

- Sunday: 11.00am and 6.30pm
- Open Tuesday 9.30am–2.00pm

68 ABERFOYLE PARISH CHURCH

**Loch Ard Road
Aberfoyle
FK8 3SZ**

A NN 518 005

Church of Scotland

Linked with Port of Menteith

On the B829.

John Honeyman designed this church which sits at the foot of Craigmore and on the banks of the River Forth. In early-Gothic style 1870, it replaced the old kirk of Aberfoyle on the south bank of the river reached by crossing the humpback bridge. The new church was enlarged in 1884 to include transepts. The interior is elegant with the minimum of ornamentation. Magnificent roof timbers. Stained glass, including a window by Gordon Webster 1974. Two-manual pipe organ 1887 by Bryceson Brothers, London.

- Sunday: 11.15am
- Open July and August, Wednesday 2.00–4.00pm, or by arrangement (01877 382391)

CLACKMANNAN / STIRLING

69 ST MARY'S, ABERFOYLE

Main Street
Aberfoyle
FK8 3UJ

NN 524 010

Scottish Episcopal

www.stmarychurchaberfoyle.
org.uk

**Linked with St Andrew's
Callander**

This small rural church was designed
by James Miller, who also designed
Gleneagles Hotel. It was built 1892–3
by workers from the local slate quarry
using stone from Ailsa Craig brought
by railway (free of charge) to test the
weight capacity of the new branch
railway. Charming Arts & Crafts style
with pale harling and red sandstone
dressings. Oak-panelled reredos.
Organ by Henry Willis.

• Sunday: 11.15am Eucharist
• Open by arrangement (01877 382611)

70 BALQUHIDDER PARISH CHURCH

Balquhidder
FK19 8PA

NN 536 209

Church of Scotland

Linked with Killin

Handsome parish church in dressed
stone, built 1853 by David Bryce.
Exhibition of the history of the
church. Bell donated by Rev. Robert
Kirk (1644–92), a notable boulder
font and the supposed gravestone of
St Angus, possibly 9th century. The
ruins of the old parish church are in
the graveyard where there are many
intriguing carved stones, including
that of Rob Roy MacGregor.

• Sunday: 12.00 noon
◦ Sunday evening concerts during
  summer months
• Open daily

STIRLING

71 OUR LADY & ST NINIAN'S, BANNOCKBURN

**Quakerfield
Bannockburn
FK7 8HZ**

⚔ NS 813 903

⛪ Roman Catholic

🌐 www.ourladyandstninian.org.uk

Linked with Sacred Heart Cowie

Archibald Macpherson 1927, in a modified Early Christian style. Built in multicoloured bricks with a red tiled roof and a copper spire. Grey brick interior with wide-arched arcades and open timber ceiling. Stained glass windows.

• Saturday Vigil: 6.30pm; Sunday: 12.00 noon; Tuesday and Thursday: 10.00am
• Open by arrangement (01786 812249)

72 BRIDGE OF ALLAN PARISH CHURCH

**Holy Trinity
12 Keir Street
Bridge of Allan
FK9 4NW**

⚔ NS 791 974

⛪ Church of Scotland

🌐 www.bridgeofallanparish
church.org.uk

Corner of Fountain Road.

Built in 1860 and enlarged later, the church contains chancel furnishings designed in 1904 by the eminent Scottish architect, Charles Rennie Mackintosh. The church has an attractive timber roof and excellent stained glass windows by Kempe family, Ballantine and Adam. Organ by Lewis, 1884, with additions. New halls, 2008, of environmentally friendly design and materials with ground-source heat pump.

• Sunday: 11.00am
• Saturday, June to August 10.00am–4.00pm, or by arrangement (01786 834155)

73 ST SAVIOUR'S, BRIDGE OF ALLAN

**Keir Street
Bridge of Allan
FK9 4AT**

 NS 792 973

Scottish Episcopal

www.stsaviour.org

Corner of Fountain Road.

Church adjacent to rectory 1857, architect John Henderson, and later enlarged 1871–2 by Alexander Ross. Hall added to rectory 1893. Vestry added 1928. Gothic style with tall roof and belfry. West window by Robert Anning Bell, Stephen Adam Studio, 1922.

- Sunday: Said Eucharist 8.00am, Sung Eucharist 10.00am
- Open generally 10.00am–5.00pm

74 ST ANDREW'S, CALLANDER

**Leny Road
Callander
FK17 8BA**

NN 625 081

Scottish Episcopal

www.standrewschurchcallander.org.uk

Linked with St Mary's Aberfoyle

Sheltered by a magnificent cedar of Lebanon, this pretty little church was consecrated in 1857. The architects were either J. J. W. & W. H. Hay or 'the stonemason at Stronvar' who worked on the parish church at Balquhidder for David Bryce in 1853. Enlarged by the addition of transepts in 1886. Organ by Abbot & Smith of Leeds 1898.

- Sunday: 10.00am; Wednesday: 10.00am
- Open by arrangement (01877 330798)

STIRLING

76 DUNBLANE CATHEDRAL

The Cross
Dunblane
FK15 0AQ

NN 782 014
Church of Scotland
dunblanecathedral.org.uk

One of Scotland's noblest medieval churches, the lower part of the tower is Romanesque, but the larger part of the building is of the 13th century. Six late 15th-century choir stalls survive. The Cathedral was restored by Sir Robert Rowand Anderson between 1889 and 1893. Screen, pulpit, lectern and font by Anderson. Choir stalls and organ case by Sir Robert Lorimer. Important ensemble of stained glass by Clayton & Bell, Gordon Webster, Douglas Strachan, C. E. Kempe and six magnificent choir windows by Louis Davis.

- Sunday: 9.15am and 10.30am (winter); 9.15am only (summer)
- Open April to September: Monday to Saturday 9.30am–6.30pm, Sunday 1.30–6.30pm; October to March: Monday to Wednesday 9.30am–4.30pm, Thursday 9.30am–12.30pm, Saturday 9.30am–4.30pm, Sunday 2.00–4.30pm

75 SACRED HEART CHURCH, COWIE

Main Street
Cowie
FK7 7BN

NS 836 890
Roman Catholic
www.ourladyandstninian.org.uk

Linked with Our Lady Bannockburn

In a rural hilltop setting, a red brick church by Reginald Fairlie, 1937. A pyramid-slated octagon with projecting porch and sanctuary. Inside, steel lattices support the roof structure. Sanctuary floor and altars in variegated marbles.

- Sunday: 10.30am; Monday and Friday: 10.00am
- Open by arrangement (01786 812249)

77 ST BLANE'S CHURCH, DUNBLANE

High Street
Dunblane
FK15 0ER

🏛 NN 783 013

⛪ Church of Scotland

🌐 www.stblaneschurch.org.uk

Junction with Sinclairs Street Lane.

Open 1854 as Free Church which through unions became East United Free Church and East Church of Scotland. United with former Leighton Church in 1952 to become St Blane's Church. Stained glass includes windows from Leighton Church, other windows by Roland Mitton. Interesting tapestries in vestibule including a reproduction of *The Light of the World* by Holman Hunt. Pipe organ 1860 by Peter Conacher, perhaps the earliest example of his work in Scotland.

- Sunday: 11.15am (10.15am June to August), and 6.30pm
- Open by arrangement (01786 822268 or 01786 822657 or 01786 822142)

78 ST MARY'S EPISCOPAL CHURCH, DUNBLANE

Perth Road
Dunblane
FK15 0HQ

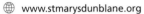

🏛 NN 784 013

⛪ Scottish Episcopal

🌐 www.stmarysdunblane.org

Built 1845, in simple early Gothic style by John Henderson, St Mary's is a community church combining prayer, worship, social action, fun and compassion with a strong interest in the nurture of children and young people. Richly carved stone font, pulpit and altar. Stained glass by James Hogan of James Powell & Sons. Pipe organ 1845 by Wood, rebuilt using original pipes by Binns, Fitton & Haley.

- Sunday: 8.30am and 10.30am; 1st Thursday of the month: 10.30am
- Garden Fête, last Saturday in August
- Open daily 9am–5pm

79 CHURCH OF THE HOLY FAMILY, DUNBLANE

**Claredon Place
Dunblane
FK15 9HB**

⚐ NN 780 006

⛪ Roman Catholic

🌐 http://holyfamilydunblane.
googlepages.com

Designed by Reginald Fairley, this church was erected in 1935 by the Honourable Mrs Margaret Stirling in memory of her husband, General Archibald Stirling of Keir. Romanesque style with stone exterior and white rendered interior. Stained glass windows by Shona McInnes in memory of the victims of the Dunblane School Incident in 1996 with the theme of the triumph of light over darkness, of good over evil.

• Saturday Vigil: 5.00pm; Sunday: 11.00am; daily 10.00am
• Open daily 10.00am–5.00pm

 80 SCOTTISH CHURCHES HOUSE CHAPEL, DUNBLANE

**Kirk Street
Dunblane
FK15 0AJ**

⚐ NN 783 014

⛪ Ecumenical

🌐 www.scottishchurcheshouse.org

Opposite Cathedral.

Uncovered in 1961 during restoration of buildings which became Scottish Churches House. Medieval in origin, possibly a chapel of one of several ecclesiastical residences which then surrounded the cathedral. Fine barrel-vaulted roof. Restored for use as the chapel of Scottish Churches House, an ecumenical conference house and retreat centre.

• Daily House Prayers: 9.00am
○ Programme of events, and retreats available
• Open at all times

81 FINTRY KIRK

Fintry
G63 0XG

NS 627 862

Church of Scotland

In Fintry village.

The present church, built in 1823, was constructed around the original kirk of 1642, and the congregation continued to worship in the old sanctuary while building went on around them! On completion, the inner church was demolished. The bell was transferred from old to new and is still in use today. Early 20th-century stained glass, including a First World War memorial window. Session House in the kirkyard added 1992.

- Sunday: 10.00am
- Open Easter Saturday, and Saturdays May to September, 2.00–4.00pm

82 GARGUNNOCK PARISH CHURCH

Manse Brae
Gargunnock
FK8 3AY

NS 707 943

Church of Scotland

www.gargunnock.com

8km (5 miles) west of Stirling.

Situated in very beautiful rural location. Village church of 1628 on pre-Reformation foundation, altered 1774 and with internal renovations in 1891, 1950s and 1960s. Three individual outside stairs to three separate lairds' lofts. Two good 20th-century stained glass windows. War memorial by Lorimer. Mountain indicator. Graveyard.

- Sunday: 11.30am September to May; 10.30am July and August jointly with linked churches, see notice board
- Open by arrangement (01786 860321 or 01786 860678)

83 KILLIN & ARDEONAIG PARISH CHURCH

**Main Street
Killin
FK21 8UW**

NN 573 332

Church of Scotland

Linked with Balquhidder

At the eastern end of the village.

Distinctive white-harled octagonal classical church built in 1744 by the mason Thomas Clark to a design by John Douglas of Edinburgh. Inside it has been altered from a 'wide' church to a 'long' church. The Fillan Room, a small chapel for prayer in the tower, was created in 1990. In front of the church is a monument to Rev. James Stewart (1701–89), minister of Killin, who first translated the New Testament into Scots Gaelic (published 1767).

- Sunday: 10.00am
- Open May to October during daylight hours

 84 KIPPEN PARISH CHURCH

**Fore Road
Kippen
FK8 3DT**

NS 650 948

Church of Scotland

Built 1827 by William Stirling, extensively redesigned between 1924 and 1928 by Reginald Fairlie and Eric Bell. Exceptionally graceful, Latinate in style, and incorporating a splendid and perfectly combined display of (mainly) 20th-century Christian art, including works by Sir Alfred Gilbert, Alfred Hardiman, James Woodford and Henry Wilson, as well as local craftsmen. Stained glass by Herbert Hendrie.

- Sunday: 11.30am
- Open 9.00am–4.30pm (dusk in winter)

  (by arrangement)

85 PORT OF MENTEITH CHURCH

Port of Menteith
FK8 3RA

NN 583 012

Church of Scotland

Port of Menteith

Linked with Aberfoyle

On B8034 beside the Lake Hotel.

On the shore of the Lake of Menteith, a church built in 1878 to designs by John Honeyman on a site of earlier churches with medieval connections. Simple rectangular plan, Gothic style, with square tower containing carillon of eight bells. Remarkable trefoil window by Stephen Adam. Surrounded by a graveyard and a few minutes' walk from the ferry to Inchmahome where the ruined 13th-century Augustinian Priory may be visited.

- Sunday: 10.00am
- Open July and August, Wednesday, Thursday and Friday 2.00–4.00pm

 86 CHURCH OF THE HOLY RUDE, STIRLING

St John Street
Stirling
FK8 1ED

NS 792 937

Church of Scotland

www.holyrude.org

Linked with Allan Park South Stirling

Near Stirling Castle.

The original parish kirk of Stirling, used for the coronation in 1567 of James VI, at which John Knox preached. Largely built in 15th and 16th centuries. Medieval open-timbered oak roof in nave. Choir and apse added in 1555, the work of John Coutts, one of the greatest master masons of the later Middle Ages. Notable stained glass by Adam & Small, Ballantine, Cottier, W. & J. J. Keir, McCartney, Strachan, Wailes. Largest pipe organ in Scotland, built by Rushworth & Dreaper 1940 and rebuilt 1994. Oak choir stalls and canopies 1965. Historic graveyard.

- Sunday: 11.30am January to June, 10.00am July to December
- Venue for many concerts
- Open May to September 11.00am–4.00pm

87 CHAPEL ROYAL, STIRLING CASTLE

**Stirling Castle
Stirling
FK8 1EJ**

 NS 790 941

Non-denominational

www.historic-scotland.gov.uk

There has been a chapel in the castle since at least 1117. It became the Chapel Royal of Scotland in the time of James IV in about 1500. The present building was built in 1594 by James VI for the baptism of Prince Henry. It was redecorated in 1629 in advance of the visit in 1633 of Charles I. After being subdivided to serve military uses, there was a first phase of restoration in the 1930s, and the latest phase of work was completed in 1996. A large rectangular building with Renaissance windows and a central entrance framed by a triumphal arch along its southern front. Notable features include decorative paintings of 1629 by Valentine Jenkin, a modern wagon ceiling reflecting the profile of the original, and modern furnishings including a communion table cover designed by Malcolm Lochhead.

- Services by arrangement
- Open April to October 9.30am–6.00pm; November to March 9.30am–5.00pm

 (Castle restaurant)

88 ALLAN PARK SOUTH CHURCH, STIRLING

**Dumbarton Road
Stirling
FK8 2LQ**

NS 795 933

Church of Scotland

Linked with Church of the Holy Rude

Peddie & Kinnear 1886 with the interior modernised for the centenary in 1986 by Esmé Gordon. Radical change under consideration to bring interior and grounds to the requirements of the 21st century. Two large circular and three smaller stained glass windows to commemorate the fallen in the two World Wars, the ministry of the Rev. Alan Johnston and members of the Kinross family.

- Sunday: 10.00am January to June, 11.30am July to December; Tuesday, Wednesday and Friday 11.30am–2.30pm
- Open by arrangement, contact Church Secretary (01786 471998)

89 HOLY TRINITY CHURCH, STIRLING

Albert Place
Stirling
FK8 2QL

⚑ NS 793 934

⛪ Scottish Episcopal

🌐 www.holytrinitystirling.org

One of Sir Robert Rowand Anderson's most distinctive churches 1878, close to Stirling Castle, old town and shops. In Anderson's signature Early Gothic style of nave with aisles and chancel in stone with slate roof. Polychrome brick and tiled walls and tiled floor give colour to the interior. Altar and reredos by C. E. Kempe, 1878, chancel screen by Robert Lorimer, 1922. Stained glass by James Ballantine & Son, Burlison & Grylls, Margaret Chilton and J. C. Bewsey. Conacher organ, 1878, rebuilt by Binns, 1935, and again by David Loosely, 1981.

- Sunday: Eucharist 8.30am and 10.30am, Evening Prayer 6.30pm; Friday: 11.00am
- Open Saturdays in August and September 12 noon–4.00pm, or by arrangement

90 LOGIE KIRK, STIRLING

Blairlogie, Stirling
FK9 4LB

⚑ NS 829 968

⛪ Church of Scotland

🌐 www.logiekirk.co.uk

A91, 6.4km (4 miles) north-east of Stirling.

The tower, square and pedimented and surmounted by an octagonal belfry, was designed by William Stirling of Dunblane 1805. The remainder of the church is an elegant whinstone box, by McLuckie & Walter of Stirling 1901. Stained glass windows include one by C. E. Kempe and two modern windows by John Blyth. Fourteen oak panels depicting scenes from the Bible enclose the chancel and pulpit. The ruined Old Kirk of Logie, with its good selection of 17th- and 18th-century gravestones (the restoration of which is being sought by Logie Old Graveyard Group), is nearby. In idyllic rural setting at foot of Dumyat and in the shadow of the Wallace Monument.

- Sunday: 11.00am
- See website
- Open Sundays, July and August 2.00–5.00pm, or by arrangement (01786 475414)

ST MARK'S, STIRLING

**Drip Road
Raploch
Stirling
FK8 1RE**

NS 792 946

Church of Scotland

Junction with Menzies Drive.

Original Gothic-style hall and church built in 1938 using stone from Auchinlea. The present church was built next door and opened in 1966. Five stained glass windows: *Good Shepherd, Suffer Little Children, Christ the Pathfinder, Winged Lion of St Mark, Martha*. Other furnishings gifted to the church are the pews, organ, font and lectern.

• Sunday: 11.00am
• Open by arrangement (01786 473716)

 ST MARY'S CHURCH, STIRLING

**15 Upper Bridge Street
Stirling
FK8 1ES**

NS 794 940

Roman Catholic

Nave-and-aisles Gothic Revival church by Pugin & Pugin, 1904, in red Dumfriesshire sandstone with crisp details. Lofty vaulted interior – 15m (50ft) from the floor to the apex of the roof. The shafts supporting the main ribs of the roof rest on corbels beautifully carved as angels playing on various musical instruments. Furnishings of rich pine and pews of American oak. The church is lit by eleven aisle and fourteen clerestory windows.

• Saturday Vigil: 6.15pm, Sunday Mass: 11.30am; Weekday Mass: 10.00am
• Open by arrangement (01786 473749)

STIRLING

93 ST NINIAN'S OLD, STIRLING

Kirk Wynd
Stirling
FK8 1EA

A NS 793 937
🏠 Church of Scotland

Only the tower and bell of 1734 survive following desecration of the nave by Cromwellian troops and an explosion of munitions stored in the 13th-century church by Jacobites. Present building is of 1751 with remodelling 1937 by A. A. McMichael. Interior restored and remodelled in 1960s.

• Sunday: 10.30am and 6.30pm (2nd Sunday in March, June, September and December)
• Open by arrangement (01786 813335)

 (steeple) C (hall)

94 VIEWFIELD PARISH CHURCH, STIRLING

Irvine Place
Stirling
FK8 1HF

A NS 795 938
🏠 Church of Scotland

The present building, seating 600, was erected in 1860 to replace the 1752 meeting house. The congregations have been part of the Secession of 1733, going through United Presbyterian and United Free Churches until joining the Church of Scotland in 1929. Interior largely as constructed, though the window of the creation story behind the pulpit is a modern intervention by Christian Shaw.

• Sunday: 11.00am
• Open by arrangement (01786 475961)

ST ANDREW'S PARISH CHURCH, BO'NESS

**Grange Terrace
Bo'ness
EH51 9DS**

🏹 NT 006 813

⛪ Church of Scotland

🌐 www.standonline.org.uk

Cruciform church with a combination of Gothic and Art Nouveau details built in 1904–6 by J. N. Scott and A. Lorne Campbell. Stained glass windows include *The Sermon on the Mount* by Oscar Paterson and *The Ascension* by James H. Leat. It is a vibrant congregation with worship to encompass all styles; truly a church without walls serving local, national and international ministries.

- Sunday: 10.30am and 6.30pm; Wednesday: 10.00am
- Open Monday to Friday 9.00am– 5.00pm

 ST CATHERINE'S CHURCH, BO'NESS

**Cadzow Crescent
Bo'ness
EH51 9AZ**

🏹 NS 999 812

⛪ Scottish Episcopal

🌐 stcstm.org

Linked with St Mary's Grangemouth

Off Dean Road, adjacent to Douglas Park.

The congregation was formed in 1888 and moved to the present building in 1921. Charming miniature Neo-Norman church by Dick Peddie and Walker Todd. The hall was added in 1928. The sanctuary windows depict the children of the Bible. Organ by Miller of Dundee.

- Sunday: 11.30am Sung Eucharist; Wednesday: 10.15am Said Eucharist
- Open by arrangement (01324 482438)

FALKIRK

FALKIRK

97 CARRIDEN PARISH CHURCH, BO'NESS

**Carriden Brae
Carriden
Bo'ness
EH51 9SL**

🗡 NT 019 812

⛪ Church of Scotland

The first church of Carriden was consecrated in 1243 by Bishop David de Bernam, although it is believed that the parish goes back to the time of St Ninian, AD c.396. The present church is the third. Designed by Peter MacGregor Chalmers 1909, in simple Romanesque style with a west tower and stone spire. The bell was cast in Rotterdam, Peter Oostens 1674. Inside, a wooden sailing ship, *The Ranger,* hangs from the barrel-shaped pitch-pine roof. Six-bay nave. Baptistry chapel with a wall painting thought to be of the Scottish School. Sounding board on north wall 1655. A fine stone arcaded baptismal font, two-manual pipe organ moved from the John Knox Church, Gorbals after the Blitz of 1941.

- Sunday: 11.15am
- Open by arrangement (01506 822141)

98 ST JOSEPH'S, BONNYBRIDGE

**30 Broomhill Road
Bonnybridge
FK4 2AN**

🗡 NS 828 797

⛪ Roman Catholic

 🌐 www.stjosephsbonnybridge.co.uk

Built in 1925, the church is set in its own grounds and uses the slope to rise above its halls. The colours of the rendered brickwork blend with the colours in the garden. The design brings elements of Spain, with the dramatic double stair leading to the main door, and of Italy with the bell-tower. The interior of the church is very light and gives views through the windows to the distant hills

- Saturday Vigil: 6.00pm; Sunday: 11.00am; Tuesday: 7.00pm; Wednesday, Thursday and Friday: 9.30am; Saturday: 10.00am
- Open by arrangement (01324 812417)

99 BRIGHTONS PARISH CHURCH

**Main Street
Brightons
FK2 0JP**

🅰 NS 928 778

⛪ Church of Scotland

🌐 www.brightonschurch.org.uk

6.4km (4 miles) south of Falkirk.

Gothic-style church with three-bay façade with lancet windows and small steeple built in 1847 to a design by Brown & Carrick of Glasgow. Local quarry owner Alexander Lawrie gifted the stone to build the church. T-plan, side galleries added in 1893. Chancel area modernised 1935. Windows 1993 by Ruth Golliwaws of New Orleans, USA.

- Sunday: 11.00am and 1st Sunday September to May, 6.00pm
- Open for prayer, September to June, Thursday 10.00am–12.00 noon

100 FALKIRK OLD & ST MODAN'S

**Manse Place
Falkirk
FK1 1JN**

🅰 NS 887 800

⛪ Church of Scotland

🌐 www.fosm.info

Off High Street.

There has been a Christian church on this site for 1200 years; local legend links the earliest foundation with the Celtic St Modan in the 6th century. The body of the church dates from 1811, although 12th-century pillars remain in the vestibule and the gable marks of the earlier nave and chancel are visible. The bell-tower was built in 1738 by William Adam and houses thirteen bells. Pipe organ 1892 by Foster & Andrews. 12th-century sanctuary cross. Two stained glass windows by Christopher Whall, others by Ballantine & Allen. Major refurbishment in the 1960s.

- Sunday: 11.15am
- Open Monday to Friday 12.00 noon–2.00pm

(12.00 noon–2.00pm in hall)

FALKIRK

101 FALKIRK FREE CHURCH

**Beaumont Drive
Newcarron
Falkirk**

FK2 8SN

⚔ NS 884 826

🏠 Free Church of Scotland

🌐 www.falkirkfreechurch.com

The present congregation began in 1991 and moved into its new building in 1998. The modern, spacious building, of buff brick with a red tiled roof, was extended in 2004, and reflects modern architecture but maintains a spiritual and practical ambience.

- Sunday: 11.00am and 6.30pm; Prayers: Wednesday and Saturday 7.30pm, Saturday 7.00pm
- Open by arrangement (01324 631008)

102 CHRIST CHURCH, FALKIRK

**Kerse Lane
Falkirk
FK1 1RX**

⚔ NS 893 800

🏠 Scottish Episcopal

🌐 www.christchurchfalkirk.org.uk

An early work of Sir Robert Rowand Anderson, built 1863–4, this is a small and compact church of nave and chancel but which seats 120 comfortably. The interior of yellow brick banded with red has seen some alterations but has retained its charm. Modern reredos. Visconti electronic organ.

- Sunday: 9.00am Holy Communion, 10.30am Sung Eucharist; Tuesday (1st of the month): 2pm Holy Communion; Thursday: 10.00am Holy Communion; Saturday: 9.30am Holy Communion
- Open by arrangement (01324 623709)

Ⓒ

ST FRANCIS XAVIER, FALKIRK

**Hope Street
Falkirk
FK1 5AT**

A NS 886 812

Roman Catholic

www.stfx.info

Church of 1961 to replace 1843 building destroyed by fire in 1955. Hall church with dramatic entrance façade by architect A. R. Conlin. 3.7m (12ft) statue of St Francis by Maxwell Allan. Statues of the Four Evangelists by Miss E. Dempster at the foot of tapered ribs separating five inverted triangular windows. Stations of the Cross on laminated glass panels by Felix McCullough, mosaics by Casa Group, painting of St John the Baptist by Peter Brady.

- Sunday: 10.00am, 12.00 noon, 1.15pm Polish Mass, 7.00pm; Monday to Friday: 10.00am; Saturday: 10.00am, and Vigil Mass 7.00pm
- Open 8.00am–6.00pm

 ZETLAND CHURCH, GRANGEMOUTH

**Ronaldshay Crescent
Grangemouth
FK3 9JH**

A NS 931 818

Church of Scotland

Building by Wilson & Tait completed 1911. Cruciform in plan with a south aisle and north and south transepts. Four arches support a timber barrel roof and there is a small gallery at the end of the nave. Second World War memorial stained glass window by Douglas Hamilton, Glasgow, with four lights depicting *Peace*, *Victory*, *Willingness to Lay Down Life* and *The Glory of the King of Heaven*. Willis organ of 1890 installed 1983. Memorial Chapel furnished in the south transept 1990 used for private prayer and small services. Award-winning grounds.

- Sunday: 11.15am
- Open Wednesday mornings 9.30–11.30am, March to October

105 ST MARY'S CHURCH, GRANGEMOUTH

Ronaldshay Crescent Grangemouth FK3 9JH

NS 932 818

Scottish Episcopal

stcstm.org

Linked with St Catherine's Bo'ness

The present church was built in 1938 to replace a 'tin kirk' of 1901; the architect was Maxton Craig of Edinburgh. A small hall was added in 1978. The west window, 1962, depicts the industries of Grangemouth. Altar cross, candlesticks and vases by Edward Spencer, the Artificers' Guild, his last work.

- Sunday: 8.45am Said Eucharist, 9.45am Sung Eucharist
- Open by arrangement (01324 482438)

 106 SACRED HEART, GRANGEMOUTH

1 Drummond Place Grangemouth FK3 9JA

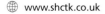

NS 930 817

Roman Catholic

www.shctk.co.uk

Linked with Christ the King Grangemouth

Corner of Dalratho Road.

Gothic Revival church, 1927 by Archibald Macpherson, with pairs of round-headed windows. Statue of the Sacred Heart above the front door in memory of the casualties of the First World War. Interior of brick with timber ceiling. Makin organ installed 2003.

- Sunday, Tuesday and Thursday: 9.30am; Saturday: 10.00am
- Open by arrangement (01324 482253)

107 CHRIST THE KING, GRANGEMOUTH

**Bowhouse Road
Grangemouth
FK3 0HB**

A NS 929 802

Roman Catholic

www.shctk.co.uk

Linked with Sacred Heart Grangemouth

A centre for all with worship at its heart. Opened in 1975 by Canon Kruger. Stations of the Cross moulded in plaster by J. Higgins showing the main symbols of Hindu, Muslim, Christian and Jewish faiths. Carved Madonna, Our Lady of the Veil, from Oberammergau.

- Saturday Vigil: 7.30pm; Sunday: 11.00am; Monday and Friday: 9.30am; Wednesday: 7.30pm
- Open by arrangement (01324 482253)

108 LARBERT OLD CHURCH

**Denny Road
Larbert
FK5 3AB**

A NS 856 822

Church of Scotland

www.larbertoldparishchurch.oc.uk

Near site of earlier chapel – 12th-century dependency of Eccles Kirkton of St Ninian's and Cambuskenneth Abbey. The present church of 1820, architect David Hamilton, replaced a pre-Reformation church which was located within the adjacent churchyard. The fine oak panelling of 1887, chancel added 1911. Good memorial windows including Gordon Webster and Stephen Adam. The apsidal triptych of the Transfiguration is believed to be the only example of Frank Howard's work (1805–66) in Scotland and was executed by Edmundson of Manchester. Interesting memorial plaques. The graveyard includes the burial place of James Bruce, Abyssinian explorer, and Master Robert Bruce, the post-Reformation divine, as well as the early partners of the Carron Company. The bell-tower has a carillon of chimes dating from 1985.

- Sunday: 11.00am and 6.30pm
- Open by arrangement (01324 562955)

 (church) (churchyard)

109 OUR LADY OF LOURDES & ST BERNADETTE, LARBERT

**323 Main Street
Larbert
FK5 4EU**

NS 865 829

Roman Catholic

The present building designed by J. N. Scott & A. Lorne 1934 was intended to be a hall but was used for worship until a permanent church could be built. When this plan was abandoned in the 1950s the building was adapted to become exclusively the place of worship. Entrance porch by Sam Sweeney added 1995. Wall hangings by Maison Bouvrier 2002. Marian Grotto in grounds 1983 to mark the Golden Jubilee, recently embellished and decorated by local talent from within the church community.

- Sunday: 11.30am and 6.30pm; weekdays: 9.30am; Thursday: 7.30pm
- Open 9.00am–dusk or by arrangement, contact Presbytery (01324 553250)

110 STENHOUSE & CARRON PARISH CHURCH, STENHOUSEMUIR

**MacLaren Memorial Church
Church Street
Stenhousemuir
FK5 4BU**

NS 876 831

Church of Scotland

Built 1897–1900 with linked Manse, 1906, architect J. J. Burnet, the assembly is dominated by the massive square tower and timbered porch. The silvered-bronze font of 1900 is by Albert Hodge and the pipe organ of 1902 by J. J. Binns. The communion table, 1921, was designed by J. J. Burnet and carved by Wylie & Lochhead with figures by William Vickers. Stained glass by Douglas Strachan from 1914, 1922, 1937 and 1950. New window, 2005, to celebrate Year of the Eucharist.

- Sunday: 11.15am
- Open by arrangement (01324 562688)

111 ABERCORN KIRK

Abercorn
EH30 9SL

NT 082 792

Church of Scotland

Off A904, 0.8km (½ mile) west of Hopetoun House.

The kirk probably occupies the site of a 7th-century monastery founded by Lindisfarne Priory. The building dates from 11th century and has a fine 12th-century south door. The Duddingston burial aisle 1603, Binns aisle 1618, Philipstoun burial enclosure 1723 and Hopetoun aisle 1707 have fine mural monuments. Interior remodelled by Peter MacGregor Chalmers 1893, except for the splendid Hopetoun Loft of 1707 designed by William Bruce with carving by William Eizat and a heraldic ceiling by Richard Waitt.

- Sunday: 10.00am
- Open daily

 (by arrangement)

112 ST COLUMBA'S, BATHGATE

79 Glasgow Road
Bathgate
EH48 2AJ

NS 967 688

Scottish Episcopal

www.stcolumbasbathgate.co.uk

Design by W. J. Walker Todd & Millar in 1915, the church is of rectangular plan with reduced chancel with organ recess off. The principal elevation is a pitched roof swept down over ancillary accommodation. Square tower over the vestry and a stone gabled and arched entrance to the west. Alterations and extension 1998. Triptych in the apse by local artist Mabel Dawson, said to be presented by Lady Baillie.

- Sunday: 11.15am
- Open Wednesday mornings 10.00am–12.00 noon, or by arrangement (01506 842384)

WEST LOTHIAN

WEST LOTHIAN

113 BOGHALL PARISH CHURCH

**Elizabeth Drive, Boghall
Bathgate
EH48 1JB**

⚐ NS 996 686

⌂ Church of Scotland

The building of this dramatic modern church by Wheeler & Sproson was started in 1960 and completed in 1965. The sanctuary seats 400 and has a unique hyperbolic paraboloid roof finished internally with timber. Windows with plain coloured glass between the roof and the walls light the interior. The church received full status in 1974, previously being an extension charge. The original bellcote was recently removed for safety reasons.

• Sunday: 11.00am, evening services as announced
• Open by arrangement (01506 654440)

 114 ST MICHAEL'S PARISH CHURCH, LINLITHGOW

**Kirkgate
Linlithgow
EH49 7AL**

⚐ NT 002 773

⌂ Church of Scotland

🌐 www.stmichaels-parish.org.uk

One of the finest examples of a large medieval burgh church. Consecrated in 1242 on the site of an earlier church, most of the present building dates from the 15th century with some 19th- and 20th-century restoration. Situated beside Linlithgow Palace, its history is intertwined with that of the royal house of Stewart. The modern aluminium crown, 1964, symbolises the Church's continuing witness to Christ's Kingship. Window commemorating 750th anniversary of the church 1992 by Crear McCartney. Carving of Queen Elizabeth II by John Donaldson added to Queen's Pulpit in 2003. New organ installed by Matthew Copley 2001 from Queen Ethelburga's College, Harrogate. The Peel, Linlithgow Palace and Loch adjacent.

• Sunday: 9.30am and 11.00am
• Open all year: May to September 10.00am–4.00pm; October to April 10.00am–1.00pm

 (by arrangement)

115 ST PETER'S EPISCOPAL CHURCH, LINLITHGOW

**153 High Street
Linlithgow
EH49 7EJ**

⚑ NT 000 770

⛪ Scottish Episcopal

🌐 www.stpeterslinlithgow.co.uk

South side of High Street.

Built in 1928 as a memorial to George Walpole, Bishop of Edinburgh and his wife Mildred, with assistance from missions in England and USA. Design by J. Walker Todd of Dick Peddie & Todd is a Byzantine basilica with a 'cross in the square' plan form, a high central dome and half dome over the sanctuary apse. It is a small church, popular as a refuge from the main shopping area.

- Sunday: Sung Eucharist 9.30am; Tuesday: Said Eucharist 10.30am
- Open Tuesday and Saturday, from May to September 2.00-4.00pm, or by arrangement (01506 842398)

116 LIVINGSTON VILLAGE KIRK

**Kirk Lane
Livingston
EH54 7AY**

⚑ NT 037 669

⛪ Church of Scotland

🌐 www.livoldpar.org.uk

Close to Heritage Centre.

There has been a church on the site since 12th century. The present building was rebuilt 1732. Late 18th-century pews and pulpit with Gothic sounding board and a pretty stair. Pewter communion vessels and old collecting shovels on display. Plaque in entrance commemorates Covenanters from village who were drowned off Orkney. Kirkyard has some fine monuments from 17th and 18th centuries, including some lively headstones featuring phoenixes and leafy cartouches.

- Sunday: 10.00am
- Open by arrangement (01506 420227)

117 KIRK OF CALDER

**Main Street
Mid Calder
EH53 0AN**

NT 074 673

Church of Scotland

www.kirkofcalder.com

This 16th-century parish church, recently restored, won the West Lothian Award for Conservation in 1992. John Knox, James 'Paraffin' Young, David Livingstone and Frédéric Chopin have visited here – we look forward to meeting you too! Admission free, donations welcome. Organ by James Conacher 1888. Restoration of stained glass windows 1995. Near to Almondell Country Park.

- Sunday: 10.30am
- Open May to September, Sunday 2.00–4.00pm

118 POLBETH HARWOOD PARISH CHURCH

**Chapelton Drive
Polbeth
EH55 8SQ**

NT 029 641

Church of Scotland

www.polbethharwood.co.uk

The congregation was formed in 1795 and the first church completed in 1796 as a Burgher Kirk. Congregation translated from West Calder to the present building in Polbeth in 1962. It is a multifunctional building providing for worship and community activities.

- Sunday: 11.15am
- Open Wednesday 10.00–11.30am

 (Wednesday 10.00–11.30am)

119 TORPHICHEN KIRK

The Bowyett
Torphichen
EH48 4LT

 NS 969 725

Church of Scotland

http://thekirk.torphichen.org

Built in 1756 on the site of the nave of the 12th-century preceptory, it is a T-shaped building with three galleries including a laird's loft. Two centre pews can be tipped back to form extended communion tables. Sanctuary stone in the graveyard. Preceptory church adjoining in the care of Historic Scotland.

- Sunday: 11.15am all year and 7.00pm October to February
- Open (parish church and preceptory) Easter to end October, Saturday 11.00am–5.00pm, Sunday 2.00–5.00pm. Charge for entry to preceptory

120 ST NICHOLAS, UPHALL

Ecclesmachan Road
Uphall
EH52 6JP

NT 060 722

Church of Scotland

www.strathbrockparish.net

Tower and nave with Romanesque doorway of 1187, Buchan stairs of the 17th century, aisles added 1590 and 1878. A picture shows the balconies that existed before the restoration of 1938. Buried in the tower are Erskines, Earls of Buchan and sons. Mixture of old and modern stained glass windows. The bell, one of the oldest in West Lothian, is inscribed 'in onore sancte nicolae campana ecclegie de strabork anno dni mviii'. 'Judas' Bible of 1613.

- Sunday: 11.00am
- Open by arrangement (01506 852550)

121 **WHITBURN SOUTH PARISH CHURCH**

**Manse Road
Whitburn
EH47 0DH**

NS 947 646

Church of Scotland

www.whitburnsouthparishchurch.
org.uk

In its present form dating from 1729, the walls house a modern interior of the 1950s, the result of a fire. Cruciform and typically Georgian, though some earlier architectural features are evident. The graveyard is host to several local notables and is the last resting place of Robert Burns's eldest daughter, Elizabeth Paton (dear 'Bought' Bess) who married John Bishop, the overseer at Polkemmet Estate.

- Sunday: 11.00am all year; 1st Sunday September to May, 6.00pm; 1st Sunday in June, 3.00pm
- Open by arrangement (01501 741627)

Index

References are to each church's entry number in the gazetteer.